Tracing Your Ancestry

Tracing Your Ancestry

A STEP-BY-STEP GUIDE TO RESEARCHING YOUR FAMILY HISTORY

F. Wilbur Helmbold

Oxmoor House®

ISBN: 0-8487-0486-X
Library of Congress Catalog Card Number: 76-14109

Manufactured in the United States of America

Tracing Your Ancestry

Editor: Karen Phillips Irons
Cover Photograph: Taylor Lewis
Photographs: Gerald Crawford

Ninth Printing 1991

Contents

Introduction

Pursuing your family history is fun. If you choose to pursue a career in genealogy, there are many professional and academic requirements ahead. You may trace your ancestry for many generations by using this informative step-by-step guide to your genealogy.

You will learn to use the records in libraries, archives, churches, genealogical and historical societies, and lineage societies. Your exciting search will include checking indexes to records, examining records, and making abstracts. Your research will naturally lead to pitfalls and problems, which are also explored.

In your research, you will laugh at your ancestors and probably at yourself. But you will also learn to appreciate your heritage from a scientific viewpoint. This will lead you inevitably to a deeper understanding of the people and the world in which you live.

You will find in your ancestral line the lowly along with the well born. Each may inspire or motivate you.

I must acknowledge my profound appreciation to my wife, Neola Wood Helmbold, whose adoption as an infant and subsequent early loss of her foster parents left her with no living lineal ascendants. Her genealogical circumstances inspired me to begin a serious study of her ancestry. This study was a real test of the validity of genealogical research and of the progress that can be made under such difficult circumstances.

I must give much credit to the professional ability of my faculty colleagues of the Institute of Genealogy and Historical Research at Samford University. I should like to acknowledge the assistance of Milton Rubincam and Virginia P. Livingston, both of whom made extensive recommendations and criticisms. Also, I have been favored with the privilege of being instructed by Kenn Stryker-Rodda, John I. Coddington, and Jean Stephenson.

I have called upon numerous individuals for assistance in one way or another such as Lloyd D. Bockstruck of the Dallas Public Library, Anne D. Budd of *Ohio Records and Pioneer Families,* Richard Lackey of the *Mississippi Genealogical Exchange,* Florida B. Segrest of East Alabama Genealogical Society, Jimmy B. Parker of the Genealogical Society of Salt Lake City, Mildred Russell and Dorothy Woodyerd of the Daughters of the American Revolution, Peggy Doss of the Jefferson County Courthouse Record Room, Jimmy D. Walker of the National Archives, Alice Reinders, Arlington, Virginia, Milo B. Howard (Director) of the Alabama Department of Archives and History, Mary K. Meyer of the Maryland Historical Society, Colin James of the Colorado Genealogical Society, and William B. Halbrooks, Birmingham, Alabama.

On my own university campus, I am grateful for the encouragement of President Leslie S. Wright, Vice President Ruric E. Wheeler, Dean Lee N. Allen, Professor David M. Vess and his remarkable history department faculty, and the faculty and staff of the Samford University Library whose unfailing consideration has been extended to me on numerous occasions.

I hope that you will receive the same generous consideration in your research as I have in the preparation of this book.

F. Wilbur Helmbold

A Family History Can Be Fun

You know something of your family history, much more than you realize. Whatever your present knowledge, you need guidance and encouragement as you proceed in an effort to develop and extend the family record. Along the way you will encounter pitfalls, detours, and rough roads as you undertake the limitless pursuit of your modern and ancient relatives and their characteristics.

To challenge, to encourage, even to prod you to follow an orderly progression of research—that is what this book is all about. Many things that you learn and experience on the route will be your own discoveries. You will discover not only new names and old places, but you will get a new joy from some things that you never anticipated. During the process, you will gain not only *facts* but *meanings* from places, events, and times you encounter. It is an experience that you will not want to miss.

Before you head in a certain direction in search of information about your family history, try to determine what you will learn and what the costs will be. It is somewhat like the reading you may do before redecorating, renovating, landscaping, or gardening.

What benefits will you derive from devoting time and effort to the family history?

You will gain knowledge somewhat imperceptibly at first. This knowledge will be not only of the family itself, but of

1

the settings and events in which the family has lived. Some say that family history is the basis of all history; certainly there is substantial truth in this. The impact of major and minor events in recorded history will be perceived in the lives of the ancestors you learn about. You will gain an appreciation of those individuals' interplay with past events, and you will want to know more about the persons and events in a more direct way. You will find both early and current maps interesting and rewarding because of the migrations of your people.

You will obtain knowledge of the *social, religious, economic,* and *political* aspects of your ancestors' lives, including the mavericks and the gifted. You will be able to see the hereditary influences which make up your ancestral lifestream. You will gain an appreciation of the physical characteristics of your ancestors and of your living relatives. Perhaps you will look in your own mirror. Your family research may elicit greater self-understanding; however, you should not become too self-analyzing.

Surprisingly, you may find yourself developing a sufficient vocabulary in other languages to decipher records or documents of the family in those languages.

Thinking and Planning

If you are going to be proficient at gathering your family history, you need to develop sufficient ability to solve puzzles by analysis.

From time to time in this book I shall refer to specific examples of genealogical research to make a point. Some of these examples come from my own family research. Here is an example to illustrate the type puzzles you will learn to decipher: Working with assorted facts develops your ability to determine which John Heber in Canton County was the John Heber who had a son Samuel the blacksmith, instead of Samuel the country storekeeper. You must determine whether those Samuels are one and the same, or two different individuals. These puzzles are often encountered, and they are fun to take apart and put back together in the correct fashion.

You will learn to organize your information on the sheets or cards that you use and in the files or loose-leaf binders that you develop and increase. You must organize material, or you will get lost in the miscellany that you accumulate.

And you will quickly learn to organize your searches toward workable goals with clear focus on your *immediate objective* and its place in the larger compass of your family history. *As an example, my relative Joseph K. had a brief career in Wyoming County during the 1870s. This era was a specific goal on one research trip we made to the county.* Save time and money by defining your goals and by planning your activities well.

Happiness Is Where You Find It

Develop a healthy skepticism in the search for your ancestral history. You will encounter many silly beliefs about your family. At the same time, you will meet a lot of wonderful people, not only in your family but among other people. There will be those who are doing similar studies of their own families. There are those who will be unbelievably helpful: the lady clerk at the county courthouse (too tired to smile, but too nice to be rude), the librarian (fed up with patrons insisting on being Washington's descendants—he didn't have any), and the irascible old codger from Borhaven (who still loves any and all of the family).

The humanity of it all is bound to impress you eventually, and you will learn to laugh at yourself occasionally.

You will have a renewed desire to write, to read, to travel, and to converse. Many records that you need for the family history will be in places some distance from the family today.

You will soon be writing to these places, reading about them, traveling to them, and conversing with people there and at home. Out of necessity, you begin to improve your handling of correspondence. Once you have written for a copy of a record, you will eagerly look forward to the reply, and this will encourage you to become a better correspondent.

You will certainly begin to collect a few books, and you may acquire a great many volumes. As you progress in your historical research, you will probably learn to be more selective of the books you buy, and your library will become a partner in your project. There will be how-to books, histories of towns and counties and nations, collections of transcribed, abstracted, and/or indexed records germane to your family, and other sources of interest.

Travel becomes a delight for the opportunity it affords you to view and to abstract records and to see library collections at your travel way points and destinations.

Conversation with others becomes more meaningful and your relationships more real as you discuss your many connected families; for if your family has been in the nation or country for six generations, the present number of descendants from an ancestor could be in excess of 1,000. This is not to mention all of the families related through ancestors who intermarried with yours.

Your Family History—Bound or Unbound

Your goal may be to develop a full family history, which is satisfying and useful. You move, sometimes imperceptibly, toward that goal. You should determine the form in which the compiled family history will appear. If you can afford it, you may choose a well-printed, well-bound volume like those which you see in libraries.

You must determine the point at which to conclude your research and compilation and turn to the preparation of the typed or handwritten text for the book. You must choose what to include and what to leave out of your book.

Have fun along the way, but keep your objective in mind.

Making Your Record

Record the family history in a permanent, convenient, and orderly manner. You can devise your own forms, or you can obtain printed ones. (A convenient set in the *Tracing Your Ancestry Logbook* is available for your use with this book. Since your family history will grow more than you realize, the set is loose-leaf and matching forms are available.)

Your basic family history will include two different records: (1) Ancestral Charts (formally known as pedigree charts) and (2) Family Group Records. The ancestral charts can give you an overall view of each family line you record. The family group sheets will give you both a compact summary and details of each family group you discover and record.

To this solid foundation, you will add other work forms, supplementary records, and narrative details in order to develop and conclude your family history.

The thing to remember is that any form should be your servant, not your master. Use a form to keep things straight and to help spot the gaps or missing data on which you need to focus.

Ancestors Are People

The Ancestral or Pedigree Chart is a simple form for recording the parents, grandparents, and great-grandparents of an individual.

An important aid to placing your ancestors in their times and places on the chart is the space under the name for the birth, death, and marriage of each. Be sure to get these data and put them on your Ancestral Charts.

There are other formats that may be used for the same information (such as fan charts), but this one is probably the most common, perhaps because of its visual simplicity.

You can readily fill out this Ancestral Chart up to a point, and it is best to do so at the beginning of your family history. You will enjoy going back quickly as far as you can.

Fill out your Ancestral Chart(s) and remember these points:

† Print names and data in pencil on your Ancestral Chart(s).

† Print dates of birth and death in this manner:
21 Sept 1919 (day, month abbreviation, year).

† Leave space for first and middle names.

† Use full maiden names for females, not the married names.

Surprisingly, you may find you do not even know the exact names of ancestors of some recent generations. Your knowledge may not go back as far as you expect. But the Ancestral Chart is a record to begin with, and you will enjoy filling out the chart as you discover each successive ancestor. Since these dates and full names may possibly be at variance in different sources, use a pencil to record your data on the Ancestral Charts. Many experienced family historians and professional genealogists advise penciling and point out that later determination of adequate proof will free you to print in ink instead of creating a new chart, which could result in copying errors.

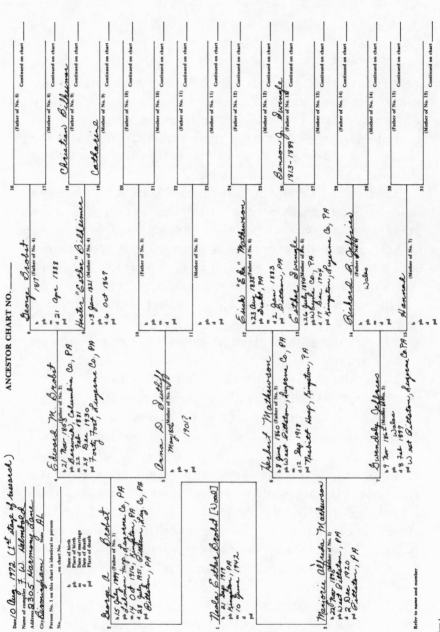

ANCESTOR CHART NO. ____

Date: 10 Aug. 1972 (1st stage of research)

Name of compiler: F. W. Helmfeld

Address: 2305 Harmony Lane

City: Birmingham   State: AL

Person No. 1 on this chart is identical to person ____ on chart No. ____

No. ____

b   Date of birth
pb Place of birth
m   Date of marriage
d   Date of death
pd Place of death

1 Nola Esther Brobst [Wood]
   b 21 Sep. 1919
   pb Kingston, PA
   m 10 June 1942
   d
   pd

2 George A. Brobst (Father of No. 1)
   b 15 July 1894, Slocum twp., Luzerne Co., PA
   pb Slocum twp., Luzerne Co., PA
   m 14 Oct. 1916, Kingston, PA
   d 28 July 1951, Slocum twp., Luz. Co., PA
   pd Pittston, PA

3 Marjorie Almeda Matheuson (Mother of No. 1)
   b 20 Nov. 1895, Pittston, PA
   pb West Pittston, PA
   d 2 Dec. 1920
   pd Pittston, PA

4 Edward M. Brobst (Father of No. 2)
   b 21 Nov. 1863, Berwick, Columbia Co., PA
   pb Berwick, Columbia Co., PA
   m 22 Feb. 1891
   d 24 Dec. 1930
   pd Forty Fort, Luzerne Co., PA

5 Anna D. Sutliff (Mother of No. 2)
   b
   pb May 1856
   d 1901?
   pd

6 Herbert Matheuson (Father of No. 3)
   b 8 June 1840, West Pittston, Luzerne Co., PA
   pb West Pittston, Luzerne Co., PA
   m
   d 12 Sep. 1913
   pd Pittston Hosp., Kingston, PA

7 Gwendolyn Jeffries (Mother of No. 3)
   b 9 Nov. 1862, Wales
   pb Wales
   d 8 Feb. 1899
   pd W. ext Pittston, Luzerne Co. PA

8 George Brobst (Father of No. 4)
   b 1817
   pb
   d 21 Apr. 1888
   pd

9 Hester "Esther" Billheimer (Mother of No. 4)
   b 3 Jan. 1821
   pb
   d 6 Oct. 1867
   pd

10 ____ (Father of No. 5)
   b
   pb
   m
   pd

11 ____ (Mother of No. 5)
   b
   d
   pd

12 Erich "Eli" Matheuson (Father of No. 6)
   b 23 Aug. 1835
   pb Scale, PA
   m 2 Jan. 1833
   d
   pd

13 Esther Burroughs (Mother of No. 6)
   b 26 July 1840, Welsh Co., PA
   pb Welsh Co., PA
   d 17 Dec. 1904
   pd Kingston, Luzerne Co., PA

14 Richard R. Jeffries (Father of No. 7)
   b
   pb Wales
   m
   pd

15 Hannah (Mother of No. 7)
   b
   d
   pd

16 ____ (Father of No. 8)
   Continued on chart ____

17 ____ (Mother of No. 8)
   Continued on chart ____

18 Christian Billheimer (Father of No. 9)
   Continued on chart ____

19 Catherine (Mother of No. 9)
   Continued on chart ____

20 ____ (Father of No. 10)
   Continued on chart ____

21 ____ (Mother of No. 10)
   Continued on chart ____

22 ____ (Father of No. 11)
   Continued on chart ____

23 ____ (Mother of No. 11)
   Continued on chart ____

24 ____ (Father of No. 12)
   Continued on chart ____

25 ____ (Mother of No. 12)
   Continued on chart ____

26 Benson J. Burroughs (Father of No. 13)
   1813-1889
   Continued on chart ____

27 ____ (Mother of No. 13)
   Continued on chart ____

28 ____ (Father of No. 14)
   Continued on chart ____

29 ____ (Mother of No. 14)
   Continued on chart ____

30 ____ (Father of No. 15)
   Continued on chart ____

31 ____ (Mother of No. 15)
   Continued on chart ____

Refer to name and number

Form 1

A Talk with Aunt Sue

Once you have filled in your Ancestral Chart, it is highly probable that there may be many bits of information you need to get. This is a good time to prepare for a talk with Aunt Sue or with anyone you think may have family information. For your talk with her you need pencils, a ballpoint pen or fountain pen, Ancestral Charts, Family Group Records, and History Sheets (or some standard-size, 8½" x 11" bond paper). Don't use yellow pads or cheap pulpwood paper. In fact, out-of-date business letterheads or surplus printed letters on good paper will do. You may prefer lined or ruled notebook paper of bond quality.

You should form the habit of writing on only one side of the paper. Put one subject, person, or family group on a sheet. It's better and more economical than making copies for different files, and it avoids miscellaneous odd-size pieces. Notes on History Sheets or bond paper should be made with pen; notes on your Ancestral Charts and Family Group Records should be made in pencil.

Family Group Records

Your family search must include all of the family, not just your two parents, and your four grandparents. Each family unit is important as a complete group. As you get further along in your research, you will discover how valuable this information is, and how necessary it is for solving problems in your line of descent.

You need a convenient way to record each complete family unit as a group; that is, the parents and their children must be recorded in the order (if known) in which they were born, along with essential details about each. This record can be kept in a narrative style, devoting a paragraph or page to each person in the group. But this method takes much space, requires much time, and does not describe the whole family together. You can avoid these difficulties by putting the information on a Family Group Record.

Note how compact this particular form is. It sets forth almost every essential piece of information you need in the course of developing your family history—birth, death, marriage, occupation or profession, and siblings (brothers and sisters) in the family. There are a variety of these forms, but they all accomplish the same purpose: to show the family group on one concise page.

Since you will have many family groups in your history as it develops, you need a number of Family Group Records. For example, you need one for your parents and your siblings, one for each of your married siblings and his family, one for your paternal grandparents and their entire family of children, and one for your maternal grandparents and their entire family of children. Your basic record should be built upon the Ancestral Charts, which go back as far as possible, and your Family Group Records, which complete each family unit with parents and children.

History Sheets

Since you will acquire much additional information about individuals and customs, you need to preserve that information by taking notes on your research. Thus, a third type of record is needed as your research grows—the History. If you have a uniform system and format for your material, you will be able to arrange it and file it accurately. A handy format, recommended by some professional genealogists, is called a History Sheet.

There are important things to note about a History Sheet: The surname of the subject should be placed on the top line upper right; the given name should fall just below that; the

FAMILY GROUP RECORD

Wife			Husband
Gwendolyn Jeffries Wales ③	Name		*Herbert Mathewson*
9? Nov 1862	Born		8 June 1860 ③ West Pittston, Luz. Co, PA
	Married		1880 ? Baptist Ch?
West Pittston, Luz, Co., PA ② 8 Feb 1899 ②	Died		12 Sep 1918 ④ Nesbitt Hosp., Kingston, PA
Pittston Cemetery, PA 10 Feb 1877	Burial		15 Sep 1918 ② Pittston Cemetery, PA
Richard R. Jeffries	Father		Esick "Eke" Mathewson
Hannah	Mother		Ester Swingle
husband	Other (if any)		wife (2) Emma Bettinger, ca. 1903, Shenandoah, Schuylkill Co., PA. Had daughter and son.

Notes

① Census 1870, substantiated by will of Richard R. Jeffries, cemetery record.
② Death certificate, cemetery record, and F. C. Johnson, Historical Read, v.7, p. 187.
③ Census 1870, cemetery record. ④ Cemetery record.

Date married & spouse

#	Sex	Children in order of birth	Born Day Month Year	Where born	Died Day Month Year	Where died
1	F	Mabel S. ① Von Dyke ② Lewis (Mattoon) - lived at Caccadaga, NY	9 Aug 1882?	Yatesville, Luz., PA	28 May 1925	Jamestown, NY
2	M	Ray[mond] Herbert Ina Williams	22 Dec 1884	? West Pittston, Luz, PA / Plymouth, Luz, PA		
3	M	Edgar R. (This child not mentioned in family information. Discovered from cemetery records of the Jeffries (maternal) family. Died age 2 months.)	May 1889	Glen City, PA	28 May 1889	
4	F	Ethel Walter C. (Fox)	Aug 1890	West Pittston, Luz, PA	ca. 1935 ca. 1941	
5	F	Flossie Reuben (Williams)	30 Sep 1892	West Pittston, Luz, PA		
6	F	Marjorie Alfreda George A (Brobst)	22 Nov 1895 15 July 1894	West Pittston, Luz, PA Lehman twp., Luz, PA	2 Dec 1920 28 May 1889	

Source

By

Form 2

HISTORY SHEET

Surname: Jeffries

Given name: Martha

Date of record: November 1, 1928

Source: Wilkes-Barre Times-Leader,
Thursday evening, p. 25.

Miss Martha Jeffries Dies.

Miss Martha Jeffries, a well known resident of this section
(Pittston), died at the home of her niece, Mrs. Merle Harris,
227 Linden Street, West Pittston, following an illness of
complications.

Miss Jeffries was born in Ryumney, South Wales, 72 years
ago and came to this country at the age of 12. For the past 60
years she has been a resident of this community. She was a
member of the First Baptist Church and its Ladies' Aid Society.
She is survived by two brothers, Benjamin, of this city, and
Thomas, of Avoca.

The funeral was held this afternoon at 2:30 o'clock.
Services were conducted by Rev. M. H. Jones, of the Water Street
Baptist, and interment was in the Pittston cemetery.

Form 3

date of the recording should come next; and the source of the information last. The source is usually the name of the person who gives the information; however, it may be a book, an article, or a document. The source should be specified in detail on the source line.

It is wise to carry a supply of History Sheets and Family Group Records with you on your visits and research trips. The Family Group Record reminds you to ask for specific items of information where there is a blank to be filled in on the record. You may be surprised at how much information Aunt Sue will recall when you ask about something you need for that blank space on the form.

Now it is time to talk with Aunt Sue.

† Show her your Ancestral Charts, especially the gaps in dates and names.

† Put question marks by anything on the chart that is uncertain or at variance with other sources.

† Keep charts and notes clear and neat.

† Jot down the current date and the name of the source beside every separate family, name, or subject entered in your notes.

† Make it fun, and yet keep delving for information to complete entries on your Ancestral Chart.

† Your talk will be most enjoyable (and repeatable) if you limit it to forty-five minutes or an hour.

Stories and anecdotes are both entertaining and enlightening. Put them on the History Sheets. They will become the flesh for the bones of the Ancestral Charts and Family Group Records. Be sure to get precise dates, places, and names; they are essential to sound work.

Filing and Analyzing Your Data

When you return from your talk, start a little file, and put your notes about each ancestor in a separate folder. You will be amazed to find how rapidly these files will develop. Office file folders and a filing box or a regular metal two- or four-drawer file will do nicely.

Before you file your notes, Ancestral Charts, and History Sheets, check to make sure that they are full and clear. Type or rewrite your notes if necessary (copying errors may arise if you type or rewrite; be careful).

In your first little talk with Aunt Sue, you may have learned that it is really Grandma Emma who is supposed to know the most about the family. You will want to talk with her as soon as possible. She may be quite elderly, and she may live in another city or state. You should visit her as soon as you can; don't put it off. You need to talk with her about the earlier generations that she will likely have information about.

Now, it's time to visit Grandma Emma, who is supposed to know a lot about the family. Your objective is not only to reach back parent-by-parent as far as she can remember but also to get more complete information about each family unit. With these two purposes in mind, it takes planning and discernment on your part to keep the conversation progressing and to keep your records accurate and neat.

Take your three basic forms along. You may tape-record stories which could be the very lifeblood of the history. This type of interview should be carefully planned, but it is valuable and can preserve the rich, precise wording of Grandma Emma's reminiscences. Wisely employed, it can be a great asset.

If you can't arrange an immediate trip to see Grandma Emma, call her on the telephone. Remember that family history conversations will cause you to lose track of time; make brief calls over a period of several weeks. This will make your research easier and will produce more satisfying information.

Analyzing Your Data

Your visits with Aunt Sue and Grandma Emma will give you so much information that you will be busy for some time getting it all put in order for your developing history files. Studying the records that you obtain is imperative. Ask yourself about each entry in relation to the others.

Now you can reflect on your history thus far. Have you made a good, accurate beginning? Are you surprised with what you learned or with what you didn't know? Surprises will continue to occur, and you must be ready for them.

Do you see the most recent and the earliest gaps in your records? This is where you begin to analyze problems, to choose ways to solve them, and to set priorities for solutions.

For example, my wife's Uncle Alvin was born at Ariel, although his older brothers William and Herbert were born in West Pittston. Since Uncle Alvin was born 28 December, perhaps his mother went to visit her parents for the holidays and stayed for the birth of Alvin? Or did she visit the home of an older sister? These analytical questions suggest new areas of research to solve the puzzle.

Bible Records

Of course, be alert to the value of any Bible record, especially the records in the old family Bible. The Bible is not always as large as an unabridged dictionary; look for the smaller sizes too. It may be a standard-size study Bible or a handier size.

The family record in the Bible may be in the front, at the two-thirds point (just before the New Testament), or even in the back. Have the entire record photostated or photo-copied on permanent paper, and include the title page and date of publication of the Bible (sometimes it's on the back or verso of the title page). If the main title page is missing, look for the one in the New Testament. If no title page is found, look for the page containing a publisher's code of symbols or an edition statement (ask a good reference librarian about these fine points). Many businesses, banks, and government offices have copying machines available for use. Photostat immediately, and be sure the copy is legible and permanent. It is one of the major documents you may need for proof of the data you have collected.

Your detective instinct should show up as you study the Bible record and observe the different handwritings of the entries in the Bible. A listing of several children in identical handwriting implies the record was made at some time following the birth of the last child listed. Was the record from someone's memory? Was it a calculated guess? Was it a copy from an earlier record now destroyed?

Was the Bible printed after the dates in the record, proving the entries were not contemporary? After all, records couldn't be kept in any Bible before it was published! You should analyze everything in the family record. But it's best to keep your findings to yourself. Even relatives don't like to think that you're analyzing them or their ancestors. Before putting the Bible records away, jot down the name and address of the person who possessed the Bible and the current date. This procedure should become second nature with you when examining all records.

At this early stage in your research you must realize that not all that is printed, written, or spoken is the truth! You will learn to double-check everything.

Pictures, Letters, and Traditions
Tell the Story, Too

You will need to become a collector of photographs or an amateur photographer; printed or written names are only real to many people after they see a picture or meet an individual. Many of us have accumulations of miscellaneous family pictures. Few, if any, of them are identified with names, places, and dates.

It's time to get organized! You can find out who the people in each picture are and where and when the picture was taken. You can at least discover the year, if not the full date.

The photographs will eventually mean a great deal to you and to your family, and they should be placed in albums for easy viewing.

When you organize the photographs—which can be done from time-to-time and not necessarily all at once—don't forget to leave room for adding related pictures to the appropriate pages. Most people are eager to share pictures once they learn that you want them and will take care of them. Also, copies can be made of existing photographs so that the owners will not have to give up their originals.

Your risk, of course, is that this particular facet of the family history can become extremely time-consuming and an excuse for not doing basic research or analyzing your information.

You may be lucky enough to find at Grandma Emma's or Aunt Alice's an artifact of several generations past—the family portrait album. This may be one of those antiques with velvet or velour padded covers, clasps to hold the book together, and paneled openings in the heavy cardboard pages for the inserted portraits. Some families can still find them around, and they supply valuable pictorial material of the family's earlier days.

Old Letters and Diaries

You may also be fortunate enough to come into possession of old family letters or diaries. These items may contain far more information of genealogical value than is imagined. The date or year of a given letter may supply a valuable point of reference for an event which is not recorded elsewhere. *As an example, when Aunt Alice sent a postcard on her honeymoon at Niagara Falls, she unwittingly provided a date approximating her marriage date.*

Also, a newsy letter with details about widely separated relatives may enable you to trace generations if the localities are mentioned. This kind of information is of great value in your genealogical search.

Letters suggest relationships that are not easily determined otherwise. Problems are frequently solved through information provided by a single letter.

Diaries, a valuable source, may be overlooked if they contain no family details. A distinguished genealogist has long been frustrated by the thoughtlessness of a diarist in his wife's ancestral line. The diarist was a Baptist minister and educator whose career involved a number of places as wide-spread as Mississippi, Tennessee, Pennsylvania, and New Jersey. His diary occasionally states that a child was born in a certain year but omits the child's name. For years this genealogist has sought the names of the children that were omitted from the diary.

It is essential to note in your records the names mentioned in diaries or letters. If the names are not meaningful to you now, they may be later.

The financial accounts of family-involved businesses or social clubs may become very useful. Local store records may indicate the approximate date that a family left a community or that a death occurred. Sometimes vital records or memoranda may be noted in the account book, not for official purposes but as a matter of personal interest.

Samplers and quilts are worth examining and photographing if possible; some of these have family information in the stitching. *A fellow teacher of mine discovered a quilt in the family home after the death of a great-aunt. The quilt contained an embroidered list of her entire Sunday school class in the late 1890s. This information was especially helpful since the 1890 census is practically nonexistent because of a fire.*

Miscellaneous items in the family memorabilia may be very useful, such as testimonials and diplomas. Testimonials may contain a clue to the personality or interests of the individual. Diplomas should be examined for clues to the age, residence, and interests of the family member. Also, you may find records of club and lodge memberships, which were quite popular in the nineteenth and early twentieth centuries. These membership certificates may lead you to the parent organization, which may have retained records.

Even silverware may be of use in resolving a knotty

genealogical problem. Insurance papers are likely to be helpful. Also, property leases may provide data or clues.

All of these suggestions should indicate that almost *anything* that bears a name, date, or relationship to a family member can be useful in your research.

It is important to get information from every possible source within the family and its related families before you try to proceed to other areas.

It is imperative that you record everything you find out, even if it doesn't seem important at first.

Also, it is of great importance to analyze your information and to perceive every fact and clue that will help you to work logically with the least amount of effort.

Traditions

What can you believe and accept about the traditional stories of your ancestors? Should you keep statements or accounts of these traditions? Yes. Record such traditions, analyze them, and separate fact from legend as you gather information.

Nearly every family has traditions. Often families will have stories passed down about three brothers. The stories usually relate that one or two of the brothers settled in a specific eastern seaboard area. Another brother is usually reputed to have moved west soon after the first settlement and is never heard from again. The idea of a lost member of the family is quite prevalent.

Often there is a tradition of a lost family fortune; for the family to gain the supposed inheritance, its pedigree must be proven. Although they are seldom authentic, newspaper accounts occasionally lend an air of credibility to these stories.

A tradition may be passed on of a birth or death at sea during an immigration voyage. The dangerous and difficult conditions of shipping during the period of immigrations through the nineteenth century are sufficient grounds for exploring the possibility of a birth or death at sea.

Mention of a Quaker ancestry, or the religious affiliation of the earlier generations, is important to note for further investigation. It can explain some other circumstance in the family history, such as the absence of Revolutionary War service because of Quaker pacifism.

The religious affiliations of family members can be important to your search later, so be sure to put them in your records. A convenient method to use with some traditions is to note them on your family group sheets with a question mark after the item, for example, Methodist(?).

Traditions of Mayflower or Jamestown ancestry are so widespread and generally unsubstantiated that you may be tempted to ignore them.

Perhaps the most common misconception is that the family descended from a famous person of the same surname. For example, not all Allen families are descended from Ethan Allen, or all Marion families from Francis Marion (both Revolutionary heroes). Even the most plausible traditions regarding your family name or the country of origin must remain suspect. Concentrate on the facts about *your* family rather than doubtful traditions. It is wise to note them as traditions, and then eventually work back a hundred years or more on your ancestry before looking into such a remote possibility.

Never start back at any given point and try to trace the family down to yourself. Such an effort is a total waste of time and materials. The logical and fundamental tenet of sound work on your family history is to proceed from yourself back to each previous generation and to do it well enough so that no mistakes of importance are made. *Work from the known to the unknown.*

You will be astonished at the way some people throw aside good sense when they work on family history. Proceed logically from what you know and can prove, to what you don't know but have set out to learn and to prove.

Review the items related to a given individual or family group occasionally, and ask yourself whether they could lead to available records. Make traditions work for you. There may be a hint in any tradition that ultimately could lead to unraveling a very difficult skein of mixed information.

Records of the People and Where to Find Them

Once you have gathered everything from your family sources, both oral and written, it is tempting to begin your research at the library. Many large libraries are visited daily by hundreds of people ostensibly researching "genealogy." They are almost frenetically copying line after line of pages of "genealogy." Unfortunately, much of this is futile. You should gather facts from the wealth of county and state records rather than accumulating mounds of secondary material as a substitute.

As a university librarian of more than 25 years' experience, I have learned that genealogical research must be keyed to the original *records* concerning our ancestors. It is imperative to understand the difference between the resources of good research libraries and those of record-keeping agencies. The county courthouse and your state's vital records are essential sources for determining facts of land ownership, estate settlements, and births, marriages, and deaths. The research library will help you to determine the historical background of an area. It will also supply bibliographies and indexes to locate published material relevant to your family.

Thus, the two types of resource centers basically serve different genealogical purposes. The record agency maintains records of our lives. It keeps records of the transfer of property, the settlement of estates, and the births and deaths of individuals. The record agency is required to note all events within its responsibility without discrimination. The library usually collects materials for specific purposes and clientele.

The search for your family history is based on the evidence left behind by other family members. Thus, you must try to get proof of the events in their lives. Government records are now available for births, deaths, marriages, divorces, land transfers, mortgages, legislative acts (including private acts for the benefit of individuals), wills and administrations of estates, censuses, taxes, and military records. From these sources, a great deal of authentic and useful data may be obtained for the family history.

We are going to work with each of these in a fairly logical order. Modify your order of research when circumstances preclude your searching the next category of records in the suggested order. For example, the county records may be too far away for you to examine them, or if you are able to examine them, you may not be able to stay long enough to accomplish the necessary research. You may find it easier to take up the census search from microfilm copies at a nearby library. The census search will provide an abundance of information. You can check possible errors in the census by researching the county records.

You may have the opportunity to use the federal records that are related to military and other activities before you are able to examine the county records. However, you should not come to any conclusions from the federal records until you examine the land and estate records in the county courthouse.

Perhaps you can better use your time by reading the histories of your home state and counties. Don't be misled by inaccurate biographical accounts or by incomplete abstracts. Be cautious in accepting any information that you have not verified or that has not been checked by a certified genealogist through examination of the original records.

The progression suggested in this book is a reasonable and logical course of research. There are alternatives, but the suggested order is the most methodical approach.

Importance of Evidence

It is necessary to obtain proof of every statement vital to your family history. Proof should be pursued relentlessly and should constitute adequate legal evidence. When proof is unobtainable, you will have to settle for a preponderance of available evidence.

Every professional genealogist knows of a friend who has gathered family information which at some point lacked proof. At a certain stage of his research, he found it impossible to progress any further. Taking up the research, the genealogist soon discovered that needless work had been done on researching a family which was not related to the true family. Sometimes years have been invested and substantial sums of money have been spent on such erroneous efforts.

You should concentrate your efforts on obtaining information contained in official government records; there will be less likelihood for error. Now you can begin the process of using records to research your family history and gathering proof for all the information you have accumulated from family records.

The Proof of Birth and Death

First, you need your birth certificate and that of each of your parents. Unless you live in a city where the official agency for your state or your county is located, you will probably find it convenient to write to the appropriate agency for a copy of each of these certificates. The expense is nominal.

Perhaps you have said to yourself, "I know I was born, and my parents have told me my birth date. Why should I bother with a certificate?" Actually, you only know you are alive. Since you were not a competent witness at the time, you don't know the date and place of your birth. Your parents might not be entirely accurate about birth dates. *For example, my mother always confused April 8 and 12 for the birth dates of my two elder brothers, and they were born two years apart. The surviving brother recently obtained a birth certificate to resolve the question of which date to celebrate! You will find oddities of this sort in almost every family.*

Your nearest government bookstore may have several publications that could be useful: *Where to Write for Birth and Death Records* (.35) and *Where to Write for Marriage Records* (.30). These can also be obtained by writing the Superintendent of Documents, U.S. Government Printing Office, Washington, D.C. 20402.

Birth and death records are maintained by the respective states, and they are called state registration. Genealogists call them vital records (vital referring to life). Information given in the birth records generally includes name, date and place of birth, parents' names, ages, residence, and occupation. The death records include name, date and place of death, age, state or country of birth, occupation, name and residence of informant, date and place of burial, cause of death, parents' names and places of birth.

You can recognize the value of these records. For example, a death certificate will state the person's age, state or country of birth, and sometimes his length of residence in a community. In many instances, the cause of death is of value to you genealogically, and may be of practical value in negotiations for life and health insurance for your family. But remember that some of the facts on the death certificate could be erroneous. (For instance, the age of the deceased may not be accurate.)

You should go directly to the primary document for the record of any fact you are trying to determine; for example, consult a birth record for the correct name, date, and place of birth, and for the parents' names.

Sometimes birth certificates contain errors. *My own birth certificate incorrectly reports my mother's given name; this was due probably to a misreading of the physician's handwriting.* Many examples can be cited of similar misinformation. Information can be corrected only by other documents or sources that give dependable evidence on the point at issue. Don't panic at the thought of a possible inaccuracy on an official document. Just keep taking down all records from all sources, and these discrepancies of fact will be resolved. Southern, midwestern, and far western states were late in establishing vital registration, while New Jersey did so as early as 1848.

Marriage and Divorce Records

You will find records of marriage licenses to be helpful since they may include ages and places of birth of the couple, and names of the parents of the couple. The names may not be given as fully as in a death certificate or a birth certificate.

My wife's father gave his place of birth on his marriage license application as Lehman township; this fact should have been most helpful. Nevertheless, I have had difficulty verifying this fact because of the distance from Birmingham to Lehman township and the complete lack of family records. If the place of birth is verified, it may eventually fill a gap regarding the family's whereabouts between two censuses.

The places where records of marriages are kept vary from state to state. The clerk of the probate court is the usual source in the South and in some parts of the North, but the town clerk may be the source in New England. To write for marriage records, see the government publication mentioned earlier to get the exact name, address, and cost of copies.

Divorce records frequently contain useful information, because they deal with rulings regarding custody of children and distribution of property: this information may lead you to other avenues. In the early nineteenth century and before, divorce cases were decided by the state Supreme Court or granted by the state legislature, depending on the state. Thus, records of divorces may be found in the minutes of the respective Supreme Court or in the acts of the legislature.

Correspondence

Not many of us are fortunate enough to be within close proximity to our relatives, the courthouses, and the archival and record agencies. Therefore, correspondence plays an important role in obtaining the facts, evidence, and other records in our family research. A few suggestions are recommended to facilitate your research.

With the exception of federal and state agencies, it is customary to enclose a self-addressed, stamped envelope with each inquiry you send. This is a courtesy, and it helps to prevent your inquiry from being ignored or needlessly delayed. Libraries especially appreciate receiving self-addressed, stamped envelopes. Remember that the recipients have little time to read lengthy facts in order to understand what information you have requested. Get to the point promptly and concisely. Be courteous without lengthy apologies or commendations.

If you offer or enclose a small payment in advance for the material requested, many recipients are kind enough to refund excessive amounts.

When writing to the family members, several techniques are helpful. A Family Questionnaire form may be useful in approaching members of the family to seek their resources or information. Personalize your questionnaire with a short note written across a corner of the form; include your full name and address at the bottom. Always include a self-addressed, stamped envelope (s.a.s.e.).

Another method is often used to seek specific information about an individual or a family group. The individual is put on an abbreviated ancestor chart that shows two or three generations. Fill in a regular ancestor chart to show those few generations. Then xerox only the top portion of the chart (that you filled in) on the top half of a regular letter sheet. Include a personal note as discussed above. If you ask for specific information, you have a better chance of receiving a reply.

Sample Questionnaire

We hope to develop a short account of the family. This is not a business venture or a sales promotion. We are just interested in learning more about our families.

Would you please complete the following items if possible? We are even interested in trivial facts, since these might provide clues to further research for the family story. Use words like "perhaps" or "possibly" when you are uncertain. Add another sheet if you need to.

Please give detailed answers, specifying date, name, place, and events.

Family Bible (before 1900)
Family chart, history, or notes

Clue to family locations, such as property of any kind
Church letters of recommendation
Deeds, wills, or similar old items which mention the family
Certificates or papers from lodges, clubs, or veterans'
    groups
Military certificates, discharges, papers
Letters (before 1900) from or to family members
Marriage certificates
Old books with the family name noted
Diaries, notebooks, samplers
Old family photos, tintypes, portraits, or other likenesses
Any family stories or traditions regarding residence, rela-
    tives who served in the military, civil service, trade, occu-
    pation or profession
Any information about former homes, churches, schools,
    special events

We are interested in getting to know our family story. If
you tell us what you are interested in, we will gladly share
what we know.

Cordially,

Name/Address/City, State, Zip Code

Focus Your Research

Soon you should focus your research, because your range
of interests and surnames will become too diverse. You
probably will have to focus your research on one family line.

If travel to a distant geographic locale is necessary, you
should seek out all available records and family lines while
you are there.

On the other hand, you may need to select a comprehensive category of records such as the military records at the

National Archives, so you can work extensively through all the family lines. You may have to return several times to focus your research on one family line. Thus you avoid confusion.

Progress in your research will lead you back to further interviews with members of the appropriate family. Inquire among your family about points that need clarification. Try to discover clues to the solution of problems; continue to seek proof from records and documents within your family as well as from outside sources.

Search Control Record

A form is very helpful for keeping up with the records you have searched and the references for each family. Copies of this form are included in the *Logbook* (available with this book).

By the use of this "Search Control Record" form you can maintain a checklist of the records you search at each courthouse. You can include the indexes to the records on the same control record.

You can use the "Search Control Record" to keep track of a variety of searches, and maintain accurate and simple records of the specific library volumes which you have searched for specific surnames. You can also maintain records of searches in censuses, census indexes, tax lists, indexes to periodicals, and issues of periodicals without indexes.

You can also fill in the squares with 0 for no information found, / for information found, and X if information has been fully copied or abstracted in your files or notes. You may want to create your own system for using the "Search Control Record."

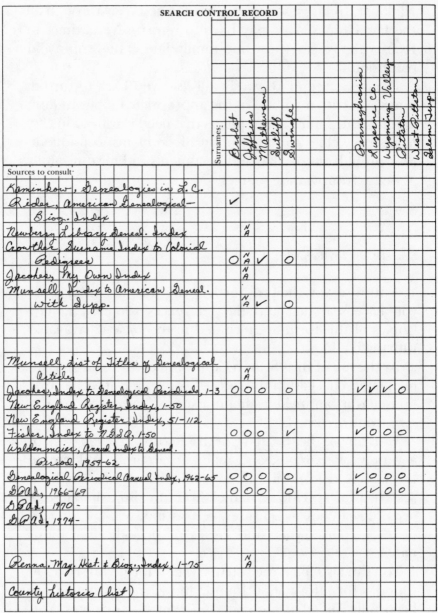

SEARCH CONTROL RECORD

Surnames: Brodt, Jeffries, Mathewson, Sutliff, Swingle

Pennsylvania, Luzerne Co., Wyoming Valley, Pittston, West Pittston, Plains Twp.

Sources to consult:

Source	Brodt	Jeffries	Mathewson	Sutliff	Swingle			Pennsylvania	Luzerne Co.	Wyoming Valley	Pittston	West Pittston	Plains Twp.
Kaminkow, Genealogies in L.C.													
Rider, American Genealogical–Biog. Index	✓												
Newberry Library Geneal. Index	N/A												
Crowther, Surname Index to Colonial Pedigrees	O	N/A	✓	O									
Jacobus, My Own Index		N/A											
Munsell, Index to American Geneal. with Supp.		N/A	✓	O									
Munsell, List of Titles of Genealogical Articles		N/A											
Jacobus, Index to Genealogical Periodicals, 1–3	O	O	O		O				✓	✓	✓	O	
New England Register, Index, 1–50													
New England Register, Index, 51–112													
Fiske, Index to N.E.R., 1–50		O	O	O	✓				✓	O	O	O	
Waldenmaier, Annual Index to Geneal. Period, 1959–62													
Genealogical Periodical Annual Index, 1962–65	O	O	O		O				✓	O	O	O	
G.P.A.I., 1966–69	O	O	O		O				✓	✓	O	O	
G.P.A.I., 1970–													
G.P.A.I., 1974–													
Penna. Mag. Hist. & Biog., Index, 1–75		N/A											
County Histories (list)													

Form 5

Pitfalls and Oddities of Family Research

You face many pitfalls and oddities in your family research. It is necessary to study the local history and geography of your ancestral settlements. You may discover the ways in which your family fits into the historic development of the community.

You may decide to join a lineage society. Perhaps you are interested in whether your family is entitled to a coat of arms. Or you may search for a doubtful legacy.

In your research, do not rely on secondary sources when primary sources are available. Remain skeptical of printed material, including the most reliable book.

Your research should begin at home; then it should branch out to the rest of the family. Undoubtedly, most of your research will be at the county courthouses where your family lived. If the places of interest are too far away to visit, first work at home to gather every piece of evidence from books, journals, and abstracts.

Learn the local history and geography of each place where your ancestors lived. Later, when you have an opportunity to visit a distant courthouse, you will appreciate the value of the original records and will use them to your best advantage. Much of your work may have to be carried on by correspondence; however, this method is very time-consuming and cannot produce the most satisfactory results.

The variety of surname spellings is a pitfall that is not appreciated by beginners in genealogical research. You must be aware of the changes in spelling that names have undergone; they were written as a particular clerk happened to hear them. As families moved, the regional accents affected the sound and the spelling of names. You should seek all of the data on the surnames in your families under every possible spelling.

You will also be surprised to discover that French, German, and Italian names are commonly found in English and Irish records. If the families of these people were in England or Ireland for several generations, a search for those surnames in France, Germany, or Italy would be wasteful until you have determined the exact identity of the immigrants. Then you should trace the families through the period of their settlement in England, before you search the records in the mother country.

Failure to Plan and Analyze Properly

You should do some overall planning; you need to set up workable goals and to decide how to achieve them. Plan each visit to the courthouse, the library, and the archives. Have objectives in your work. Plan the most efficient use of your time and sources so that you have a better chance of achieving your objectives.

Vocabulary

You will discover oddities in word usage and legal terminology. If you do not know what the record says, how can you know what it means? Upon examining the deeds and wills at the courthouse, you discover an unfamiliar vocabulary. You need a grasp of the basic legal terminology of these records.

Words that had one meaning when used one or two centuries ago now have different meanings. Junior and senior are now used to denote the father and son relationship, but they were used a short time ago to indicate two persons in the same locality with the same name, one older than the other. A man sometimes named his sons for his brothers, and thus the junior and senior in the record you are reading might be a nephew and uncle, or no relationship at all.

In-laws and stepchildren are not clearly differentiated in old records. Stepchildren may be designated as in-laws in these records. *We have yet to clarify the identity of Margaret Davies, who is designated a stepdaughter in the will of Richard Jeffries, my wife's great-grandfather.*

Cousin, brother, and sister are all terms used loosely in the South, and may mean a less direct relationship than the words imply. Personal correspondence and local newspaper references often applied these terms rather loosely. In seventeenth century records, a man might refer to an uncle, a nephew, or some other relative as cousin.

You will sometimes encounter the expression "my now wife" in wills. It means that the testator was limiting the stated inheritance to his present wife, and did not wish to extend it to a future wife if his present wife died before he did.

The words Mr. and Mrs. take a special significance in documents of the seventeenth century and in earlier centuries. Mr. was applied solely to persons of the landed gentry, to ministers and schoolmasters, and to men whose official position gave them the right to its use. Mrs. was applied to both married and unmarried women of these families.

Goodman and Goodwife were similarly used to denote persons of substance, but these people were not of the landed class or did not serve as ministers, schoolmasters, or officials of the higher rank.

Handwriting

Handwriting may not cause you any serious problems in the beginning of your family research, but you will discover peculiarities when you use the earlier records. The most common peculiarity is the use of the long *s*, commonly misinterpreted as an *f* or *p*. It is often used as the first of a double *s*, and sometimes alone, although it is seldom found at the beginning or the end of a word.

You may find it difficult to differentiate among letters with up and down strokes, such as *u, n, m, w,* and *v*. When these letters are adjacent, they are particularly difficult to read. Numbers and dates were sometimes written in a connected fashion (ligatures), which makes them difficult to read. Spellings were often transcribed phonetically; thus variations are found. Words at the ends of lines were divided by equals signs (=), or colons (:) were used to indicate the division. Capital *L* and *S* are frequently confused by modern readers; for example, a clerk in Alabama transcribed a minister's name *L*ion Blythe instead of *S*ion Blythe. Capital *T* and *F* are also confused in the swash style of handwriting. The F may usually be identified by the presence of a cross stroke on the stem of the letter. Capital *I* and *J* such as in middle initials, are difficult to identify, as neither extends below the line.

Capitalization is not uniform or consistent; it depended a great deal on the fancy of the clerk. Punctuation becomes less and less uniform as you work back in the records. Abbreviations of names are quite common, such as *Jno* for

John, *Jas* for James, and *Xofer* for Christopher. Abbreviations of words are also common, such as *exx* or *exis* for executrix and *admon* for administration. One of the commonly consulted works is E. Kay Kirkham's *Handwriting of American Records for a Period of 300 Years* (Everton Publishers, 1973).

Calendar

The year 1752 is important to remember as you begin your genealogical research. The Julian calendar was supplanted by the Gregorian calendar in the Roman Catholic countries in 1582. But its acceptance in Great Britain and her colonies did not occur until 2 September 1752. Eleven days were added to the count to compensate for an accumulation of errors in the Julian calendar. There are interesting tales about people gathering in a mob to protest the taking away of eleven days of their lives!

However, the other change made at that time is a little more difficult to perceive. Because of differing customs among the settlers, the new year began on 25 March or on 1 January. When the calendar was changed, the Parliament also established 1 January 1752 as the legal New Year's Day. Birthdays of people then had to be expressed as Old Style or New Style. For example, a date would be written as 14 February 1727/8. This means that the event took place in 1727 if the year was thought to begin on 25 March but the birthdate was in 1728 if the year was thought to begin on 1 January. Since the 25 March date is the turning point, only dates from 1 January to 24 March have to be indicated in the above way.

The Library as a Research Center and a Trap

By now someone has probably recommended his favorite genealogical library to you. Undoubtedly you have discovered rich sources and gained much material for your family history.

You may have found some published and unpublished abstracts of deeds, wills, or marriages. You have probably found the helpful indexes which provide many family names. You may have seen beautifully bound peerage volumes with impressive heraldic designs. All of these may inspire you.

Don't be surprised if you learn the abstracts are incorrect, the indexes are incomplete or misinterpreted, and the peerage volumes are insufficient without proven descent from an individual holder of a peerage. Have you ever spotted a newspaper story with a misspelled name, a misdated event, or transposed lines? This type of mistake is likely to appear in published abstracts and indexes. A library may acquire an inaccurate volume of abstracts if it happens to deal with the locale, and has a good index. You must constantly question the accuracy of all published material and seek proof from the original records.

The library will become an invaluable research center as long as you remember its place in the total research process. The courthouses, archives, and record centers are the first and final sources for your evidence. The library is the research center that you will use constantly to help you to interpret data and reorient your research.

Libraries contain abstracts and many types of indexes. You will find printed genealogies and possibly manuscript genealogies. Also, histories of countries, states, counties, towns, churches, institutions, groups, professions, and businesses are available. You can usually find city directories, maps, printed archives, printed passenger lists, genealogical and historical journals, microfilmed censuses and newspapers, and other useful reference works.

Determine what type of data you will need for your family history. As you increase your knowledge of the family, you may develop some new interest. You must then narrow the search to your immediate and specific needs for data.

Choose the library that will be most beneficial for your research problems. There are various types of libraries such as public libraries, college or university libraries, and special libraries. You will find special libraries of science, business, or of the professions. You may use all of these libraries at one time or another. Also, there are major historical and genealogical libraries available. It is impossible to do all of your research in one library; you must investigate the resources of a variety of libraries.

Choose the Best Sources

You should locate and select the best sources for each stage of your research. A reference librarian or a specialist in history or genealogy will help you locate your sources. He is professionally trained and may have considerable experience in answering difficult questions. Be humble; ask for help.

Perhaps the library has a special collection or a genealogy department. If so, the research process may be easier, because most of your sources will be in one place. The staff in a special department should be skilled in handling genealogical inquiries. However, do not confine your research to a special department: some important works may be located in the main collections of the library. Major biographical compendia and specialized encyclopedia are likely to be in the main collections.

It is important to know how other writers have described your families or their locales. Your family may be listed in a bibliography of genealogies. One kind of bibliography includes genealogies that are found in a specific library, such as Kaminkow's bibliography of the Library of Congress holdings. Regional or local lists may be available.

You should consult the bibliography published by Joel Munsell's Sons of Albany, New York, many years ago and recently reprinted. The volume lists the genealogies known to them. However, remember that some of the early genealogies will contain inaccuracies.

Also helpful are books which index individual families in various sources, such as genealogies, county histories, and biographies. The Newberry Library in Chicago has an excellent index, *The Genealogical Index,* which has been published in four volumes. You may also refer to the *American Genealogical-Biographical Index* by Fremont Rider. This is a series which is not yet complete. This work includes references to families in the 1790 census.

You may have checked for family biographies in county histories. However, you also need to read the entire history of the county. You can't understand your ancestors unless you know about their locales and their times. Be sure to study carefully the boundary changes of the counties in which your family resided. Incorrect information may appear in these histories. For example, John D. Williams in

Elmore County, Alabama, died in 1868 or 1871, according to the biographies of his two sons, but you must search the original records to determine if either year is correct. Biographies provide clues; however, the facts must be verified from primary records.

As you collect your information from various sources, you will need to remember the two keys to solving genealogical problems—place and time. Notice how this applies to the next type of source, the indexes to genealogical periodicals. If you search for the family names in these indexes, you may discover very little about the family. On the other hand, if you look for their locales, you may find more information.

The contemporary series of genealogical indexes is the *Genealogical Periodical Annual Index* (GPAI). This index lists the articles in most English language periodicals in genealogy. Unless the article deals with a specific family or methodology, the index lists it under the specific county, state, or country.

The eminent genealogist, Donald Lines Jacobus, privately published three volumes of indexes to genealogical periodicals and histories, covering the material before the GPAI was begun. This index is now published as one volume in reprint. However, there is a period of time not covered by any index.

You must not neglect bibliographies and indexes such as those on the Civil War. These bibliographies and indexes shorten the amount of time you will have to spend looking for books and articles on your subject. Observe the bibliography's publication date, and its chronological coverage. Continue your search from the date of coverage in order to identify other sources on the subject.

Indexes are of many kinds, some of which may be obscure or unknown to you. There are special indexes for specific fields such as art, music, and business. You might find useful such indexes as the index to the *New York Times*. Local indexes such as those of newspapers, church journals, and genealogical collections are helpful. Remember, the more specific in subject matter a library department is, the more likely it is to have special local indexes.

How to Keep Track

Keep track of your bibliographic and index research. Why not use the "Search Control Record" form in the *Logbook* so you can check off each family and its locale from each volume of a bibliography or index. This procedure avoids repetitive searches.

After you make lists of books and articles that refer to the family and its localities, your goal is to find these books and articles. The book or article that you want may not be available locally; however, it may be obtained from another library by an interlibrary loan. Ask your librarian to get it on interlibrary loan. It may be helpful to compile a list of references to look for if you travel to a distant library.

Biographical sketches may contain contradictory information. You must determine which account is correct.

We have mentioned only a few publications that you should consult as your research proceeds. An adequate listing of these sources would encompass several volumes. Begin with the bibliography in the back of this volume. Then consult the basic bibliography of genealogy prepared by Milton Rubincam for the Institute of Genealogy and Historical Research at Samford University in Birmingham, Alabama. This bibliography is not overwhelming, and will guide you to the basic sources. As your research advances, consult the comprehensive bibliography of genealogy by P. William Filby, published by the American Library Association. Advanced researchers will find this book indispensable. Use the bibliographies when researching a new subject area.

Card Catalog Syndrome

Books and periodicals are not the only library resources. Manuscript collections contain very useful data for research. Maps are also indispensable to your work. Microforms provide resources from distant places.

The main card catalog is almost universally used in libraries. It is important to remember that *the card catalog does not usually list everything in the library.*

The library's manuscript collections are seldom included in its main catalog. They may not even be contained in the special collection catalog. Manuscripts are usually listed in accession registers in sheet form and maintained in loose-leaf form for the current period; they are permanently bound later. There may be a special analytical catalog in the library.

Microforms owned by the library may be omitted from the main card catalog, particularly those locally produced (film laboratory of the library). Many libraries catalog microforms only if the original copy (a book or a periodical) would have been cataloged. Microforms may be listed in a separate catalog section or a microform register.

Maps owned by a library may be listed in a separate card catalog or on a special map list. Pictures, portraits, photographs, and printed archives such as proceedings of church groups or minor publications of a university may also be listed separately.

Then what does the card catalog offer? You will undoubtedly find a listing of the author, the title, and the general subject of each book. Some catalogs will include the periodicals by title or by subject and title. Individual articles in each periodical will be found through the use of printed indexes.

Biographical Resources

Perhaps the most reliable biographical compendium is *Who's Who in America,* since the information is submitted by the biographee; however, many facts may be omitted at his discretion.

Who Was Who in America does not supplant the older *Who's Who* volumes. There are individuals in the regular volumes who are not included in the permanent *Who Was Who* volumes. However, these series are restricted to leaders in government, education, religion, business, and the professions. Many other notable or popular persons such as entertainers, sports figures, and writers, are not included.

The *Dictionary of American Biography* is also highly restrictive in its criteria for inclusion. However, the *National Cyclopedia of American Biography* includes many individuals, and the biographical sketches are more complete. The information in these volumes is mainly provided by the individual biographees or their relatives. Many of the sketches for these volumes are based upon biographies and portraits supplied by the families. Thus, they are uncritical; however, many valuable clues may be found in these biographies.

A similar series entitled *Encyclopedia of American Biography* includes noncritical information. It features full page, steelplate engravings, and these volumes provide significant clues to careers, offices and events in the life of the individual. If your Uncle Andrew happened to serve as a director of a corporation or an officer of a society, you should consult the records of the organization.

The state biographical volumes that are issued by various publishers may be more useful to you. Since these volumes contain only information about the people in a single state, they are able to include a greater number of individuals from the state. It was quite popular around the turn of the century to issue state histories in multivolumed sets, of which one or more volumes were devoted to biographies. These biographies are not uniformly accurate, but they provide valuable information and clues for further research. Quite often the state archivist or a leader in the state historical organization lends his name, if not his services, to these publications.

County histories vary in their coverage, historical accuracy, inclusiveness, and format and printing quality. They should be consulted, but their content is dependent upon information supplied by the individual biographees. If an individual paid $50.00 for his book and his biography, it is likely that a flattering biography was written about him. Check the county history with the primary sources, particularly those at the courthouse.

If your ancestor was involved with a profession, a business, or a religious organization, you have to locate the biographical compendium which relates to the particular profession or religion. Doctors can be traced in the county and state histories sometimes, but the transactions of the medical society of the state in which he resided are a source that should be examined for biographies.

If your ancestor was a minister, there is a good possibility that he may have been listed in biographical or historical volumes related to his denomination. You should also examine the histories and records of the local Baptist association, Methodist conference, Presbyterian synod, Episcopal diocese, and Lutheran classis.

It is possible that information about an ancestor may be in a biographical work on the graduates of the college he attended. Historical journals should be consulted for possible information, especially if they are indexed.

Other Biographical Sources

County directories may contain biographical information and are available for some locations. City directories have been mentioned. In some areas, city directories have existed for many years; in other areas, they have been in existence only a short time. Directories of major cities have been microfilmed, and are more widely available than they used to be. A search of these directories may tell you approximately when your ancestor arrived in the area and approximately when he left it or died. Kinship is sometimes discerned by residence, even though the individuals do not have the same surnames. Occupations are often indicated, and even employers may be named.

Information in telephone directories is now fairly accurate, although they do not contain the data that may be found in the city directories. Voter lists may be helpful; they may be found in court records, newspapers, or poll tax records. School records are sometimes available.

One of the main distinctions between professionals and novices in genealogical research is the extent to which the professionals utilize the periodicals. The novice confines his searches to the surnames in which he is interested. The professional searches for information about a certain locale as well as the surnames. The information he discovers often leads him to other information.

Another distinction is the extent to which the professional knows or searches for the manuscript materials in the libraries, historical societies, and archives. The volumes of the *National Union Catalog of Manuscripts* are the major tools for finding these sources. They are found in most large libraries. Also, newspapers are invaluable sources.

You must learn to use each of these sources with discrimination and persistence. The possibilities for research are almost endless; your choice of priorities will determine how rapidly you make progress.

Research Libraries Outside Your Locale

When you are in Washington, D.C., you will want to use the libraries which have extensive collections corresponding to your subject matter. The National Genealogical Society is located at 1921 Sunderland Place, N.W. 20036, and its publications are distinguished scholarly contributions to genealogy. Its library is useful for research, and you can get helpful information about the records in other repositories in the city. Members may borrow books from the library; they may also borrow books by mail.

The innumerable resources available at the Library of Congress should never be ignored. You will find a vast number of published family genealogies, state historical and genealogical journals, city directories, land ownership maps, and books on every subject. Plan your visit carefully, and obtain a reader's permit in advance. Use your time wisely by asking only for those items that are inaccessible or not available at your local library. Use the city directories since you will not find them readily elsewhere. Also, check for the items on your bibliography that you have been unable to find. As you work toward your overseas ancestry, you will need the serials issued by societies overseas, such as those published by the British record societies.

The Daughters of the American Revolution have done a great deal to preserve the records of our people. The DAR has persistently encouraged its members to transcribe the Bible, birth, death, and tombstone records of our people. Each chapter of its organization is urged to create typed volumes of these records. At least three copies of the records are made; one is sent to the DAR Library, one to the state archives, and one to the local library. Besides these transcripts, the DAR Library has an excellent collection of county histories, published and unpublished genealogies, census records, and original mortality schedules not taken by the states.

Among their most important records are the files of members descended from those who served in the Revolutionary War. The DAR *Patriot Index* (1965) with supplements (1969 and 1973) lists the patriot, his lifespan, his spouse, his state of service, the kind of service (patriotic or military), and whether a pension claim is filed. You may request a copy of the descendant's papers. The fee is $2.00, and a copy of the file will be sent unless it has been closed by the member. If the file is closed, the member's name may be sent to you, and you may request permission from the member for the file. As a result, you may get a copy in exchange for some information from you.

Nonmembers must pay a small fee to use the DAR Library, and they may not use the library during April when members are in the city for the annual congress. The address is 1776 "D" Street, N.W. 20006.

Other Libraries

It would be difficult to discuss all of the major libraries that have important genealogical collections. We will spotlight the institutions that may be indispensable to complete and thorough research.

There is nothing quite like the New England Historic Genealogical Society at 101 Newbury Street, Boston, MA 02116. The Society's distinguished *Register* is the oldest journal of genealogy in the nation, and one of the oldest in the world. Its library is superb for New England and significant for many other sections of the country. Members of the Society may borrow books, and books may be taken out by mail.

The Genealogical Society Library at 50 E. North Temple, Salt Lake City, UT 84150, is known almost worldwide, especially for its extensive microfilming programs and its branch system for utilizing these records. A wealth of resources is available, as well as an excellent reference staff in the specialized field of genealogy.

Also, the New York Public Library has magnificent resources; this partly due to its policy of collecting every significant book related to local history throughout the nation. Its map collection is excellent, and it has extensive manuscript collections.

Each state has its own department of archives which should be consulted for materials pertaining to that state. Some of these facilities also include excellent reference collections. Some states have a separate historical library or a historical society.

Many states have county historical societies, and New York provides for a historian in each county. The local societies are often of great value because of the concentrated effort and resources on each county.

In almost every state, prominent public libraries have developed good genealogical collections. A few libraries in the South which have major collections include: Atlanta Public Library, Chattanooga Public Library, Dallas Public Library, Houston Public Library, Fort Worth Public Library, Louisville Free Public Library, Tampa Public Library, Orlando Public Library, Jacksonville Public Library, Mobile Public Library, Birmingham Public Library, and the Samford University Library (special resources in Irish history).

Libraries with major collections in the Midwest include: Detroit Public Library, Newberry Library at Chicago, Fort Wayne Public Library, St. Louis Public Library, Illinois State Historical Library at Springfield, Western Reserve Historical Society, Public Library of Cincinnati and Hamilton County, and Wisconsin State Historical Society at Madison.

A few libraries with major resources in the West include Seattle Public Library, Portland Public Library, Denver Public Library, Los Angeles Public Library, and the Sutro Branch of the California State Library at San Francisco.

A few libraries with splendid resources in the East include: Grosvenor Library at Buffalo, Genealogical Society of Pennsylvania, Maryland Historical Society at Baltimore, New York Genealogical and Biographical Society at New York, Long Island Historical Society at Brooklyn, Connecticut State Library at Hartford, Boston Public Library, and the American Antiquarian Society at Worcester.

Censuses: Their Importance and Usage

An important and commonly used source of genealogical data is the census. You have probably seen individuals using the censuses on microfilm when you have visited libraries and archives. Censuses have less evidential value than records of ownership of real property or settlement of estates. Census information is sometimes gathered from a person other than a household member, such as a neighbor, or it may be based on the census taker's personal knowledge. The census taker is frequently a temporary government employee; often this leads to careless recording of information.

Nevertheless, most censuses from 1850 include an abundance of useful information, and the earlier censuses yield helpful evidence. The censuses before 1900 are on microfilm in public libraries, college and university libraries, some state and federal archives, and genealogical societies. They are among the most accessible of all public records for your family history.

You should know a few of the major characteristics of censuses before you begin to use them. With few exceptions, these censuses are taken by counties and geographically compiled within the county. The first census taken by the Federal Government was in 1790; it was the model for the censuses taken in England and Wales decennially from

1841. The census has been taken every decade since 1790, each time with increasing detail. The censuses from 1790 to 1880 are widely available on microfilm in many libraries and archives. The 1790 census was set in type, indexed, and printed in state volumes by the government about 1906, and it was later reprinted several times by commercial firms.

The 1890 census was almost totally destroyed by fire, but a related census of Union veterans of the Civil War was partially salvaged and is on microfilm. The 1900 census has become available, and microfilm copies of both the census and its corresponding Soundex are distributed by the National Archives. These original census schedules are very extensive and therefore quite costly. Only the largest libraries can acquire the microfilms, but many other libraries will be able to acquire them as their budgets permit. Meanwhile, the 1900 census may be consulted at the National Archives or at any of its branches, which are known as Federal Archives and Records Centers. Censuses beyond 1900 have not been released.

An up-to-date summary of the type of data in these censuses is available from the National Archives (*Census Data, 1790–1890,* Information Sheet 65-224). The basic points are included in this chapter, so that you will be able to gather family information from the census. Advanced researchers should consult *U.S. Bureau of Census, Population and Housing Inquiries in U.S. Decennial Censuses, 1790–1970.* (Washington, D.C., 1973), and the latest information concerning subsequent censuses.

You should extract the data from the 1900 census first since this information will correspond to the period when your immediate ancestors were alive, and it provides useful genealogical information. Data from some later censuses can be obtained (upon submission of legal claim to the information) at the Bureau of Census office, United States Department of Commerce, Pittsburg, KS, 66762, at a specified cost (at this writing, $7.50 per entry line).

The 1880 and 1900 censuses are similar in format although advanced users will find significant points of difference. Each census gives the street and house number of city dwellers, relationship of family members to head of household, marital status, and state or country of birth of each person and of his parents; this information is in addition to the units of data required in the earlier censuses.

Each person interviewed for the 1880 and 1900 censuses was asked to state the birthplace of his father and mother. If your records take you back to the 1900 census only, you may be able to extend your family information back two or three generations with state or country of birth of two or more ancestors.

Each family member's relationship to the head of the household was stated in the census, and provides useful data. The marital status column may offer a clue to information that you've missed. Also, the street and number of the residence may lead you to information included in localized directories, school records, church records, city district directories, employment records, and perhaps the borough or community newspapers of a large city.

The 1900 census also records month and year of birth, year of immigration to the United States of America, naturalization, number of children borne by the mother, and number of living children.

Great-aunt Matilda was born in Wales in 1865 according to the 1880 census. Great-aunt Mary was born in Pennsylvania in 1867. Probably, the family immigrated in 1866. Although the 1900 census reports that the immigration was in 1865, this may be an incorrect statement.

The variations in ages, in spelling names, and other data given in the censuses are puzzling and frustrating. An authoritative genealogist has said, "You should not believe anything you read and less of what you hear, and very little of what you see!"

The 1870 census was the first to indicate Chinese (C) or

Indian (I) in the ethnic designation. Also the foreign birth of a father or mother was indicated.

The 1860 and 1850 censuses were essentially alike. For the first time, the 1850 schedules included the name of each person in the family. Other major data included age, sex, color, occupation of each male over fifteen, place of birth by state, territory, or country, and special conditions (deafness or blindness). Several other items of genealogical interest were included; refer to the detailed summary mentioned earlier. Separate slave schedules were recorded in the southern states. Since the earlier censuses did not include a detailed listing of the entire family by name, the 1850 and 1860 censuses are extremely useful.

Before 1850, the censuses named the head of the household only, and they indicated the number of other persons by sex in age groups; this arrangement varied from one census to another. Other information included the number of slaves, blind, unnaturalized foreigners, and Revolutionary or other military pensioners.

Census Indexes

The 1900 census has been completely indexed by a special Soundex system, although a small portion of it may be missing. The Soundex system, which you may use extensively in your genealogical searches, is basically simple despite its complicated appearance.

The surname is indexed by using the initial letter; the letter is followed by three numerical digits based on the consonants that follow the surname initial. Consonants that sound somewhat alike, though widely separated in the alphabet, are drawn together under one numeric code. The letters b, p, f, and v may sound alike or be confused by the hearer, and they are given the digit 1 in the Soundex system.

Brobst, Bropst, Brofest, and Brovas would all be coded B612 in the Soundex files.

The coding system is given here for you to examine:

Code	Key letters and equivalents
1	b, p, f, v
2	c, s, k, g, j, q, x, z
3	d, t
4	l
5	m, n
6	r

The vowels a, e, i, o, u, y, w, and h are not coded. Omit them when you are working out your family's Soundex codes, except as initial letters.

Remember the first letter of a surname is not coded, but is a prefix letter to the three-digit code. A name with no code numbers, as Lee, would thus be L 000. A name with only one code number would have two zeros added (Kuhne is K 500), and a name with two code numbers would have one zero added (Ebell is E 140). Key letters or equivalents appearing together (without separating vowels or noncoded letters) are coded as one digit (Barrett is B630).

Here is a sample of common and uncommon surnames worked out in the Soundex codes:

Allen	A 450	Kirkpatrick	K 621
Arnold	A 654	Love	L 100
Barrett	B 630	McCarty	M 263
Blankenship	B 452	Martin	M 635
Campbell	C 514	Nichols	N 242
Crider	C 636	Nunnelly	N 540
Davis	D 120	O'Brien	O 165
Dobbins	D 152	Phillips	P 412

Edwards	E 363	Poythress	P 362
Featheringill	F 365	Quinn	Q 500
Fisher	F 260	Rhodes	R 320
Gamble	G 514	Scott	S 230
Griffin	G 615	Taylor	T 460
Henderson	H 536	Underwood	U 536
Holcombe	H 425	Vaughn	V 250
Ingram	I 526	Walker	W 426
Jackson	J 250	Xan	X 500
King	K 520	Yarbrough	Y 616
		Zeiger	Z 260

Work out the Soundex codes for your families and have an experienced user of the Soundex verify the correctness of your coding. Then you can use the Soundex reels for the respective states in which your families were located at the time of the census. Substantial data for the Soundex cards has been extracted from the census by clerks, but it may contain errors. The 1890 fragments have also been indexed by the Soundex system.

The 1880 Soundex must be used with caution. In the 1880 census, only households in which there was a child aged ten years or under were indexed. Thus you must always consider the ages of the children to determine whether the family or household would be listed in the 1880 Soundex. Otherwise, you must search through the census of the locale where the family lived. If the family moved after the 1870 census, you must use other means to find their residence in 1880. Your persistence, patience, and analytical power will be tested. Remember, the birthplaces of the parents of each individual in the household are reported in the 1880 census.

Simpler census indexes have been produced by individuals, societies, and computer firms. To locate and to gain knowledge of these indexes requires that you consult the most recent bibliography of census indexes, genealogical periodical indexes, and card catalogs regarding this subject. Any bibliography that is now available will soon be outdated, so you should consult either a prominent genealogical library or the National Archives microfilm reading room. Even genealogical scholars have difficulty keeping abreast of newly published indexes.

Major census index projects have resulted in availability of valuable search aids. Computer-produced alphabetical census entries have been issued in bound volumes for the 1800 through 1850 censuses for all then existing states or territories. Indexes of censuses taken in various territories have been produced for: Alaska (1870-1907), Iowa (1836), Kansas (1855), Michigan (1799), (1806), and (1827), Ohio (1800-1810), and Wisconsin (1836). Indexes to adjunct source materials are also available, such as Kentucky wills to 1851, Ohio tax lists for 1800-1810, and South Carolina land grants.

These alphabetically arranged census indexes, prepared by Ronald V. Jackson and his associates, are available in many genealogical libraries. You should consult the introductions to these volumes to discover any discrepancies in indexing as well as for general information. There are errors and deficiencies in these volumes, but they are invaluable aids. However, you must verify the microfilm information of the original census schedules.

Conventional indexes were completed by Ohio researchers for the Pennsylvania 1810 census and Ohio 1820, 1830, and 1850 censuses; it was a monumental task. There are many other state and county indexes issued in various formats or published in genealogical periodicals. In your library explore the possibility of a locally produced index to a county or state census.

Mortality Schedules

As a part of the censuses from 1850 to 1880, persons who died during the twelve month period prior to the date of the census (June 1) were listed in mortality schedules. These mortality schedules include the date and cause of death as well as information similar to that listed for living persons.

If any of your ancestors died between June 1 of 1849, 1859, 1869, or 1879 and May 30 of the following year, you should find this information in the mortality schedules. Location of the schedules varies from state to state. Some of them have been published in genealogical periodicals. In Alabama, they are located in the Department of Archives and History in Montgomery. You can determine their location by consulting Stevenson's *Search and Research* or other genealogical handbooks.

In 1885, mortality schedules were prepared in four states: Colorado, Florida, Nebraska, and New Mexico. If your research deals with any of these states in the appropriate time spans, you should check the National Archives for these schedules.

State and Territorial Censuses

Regular state censuses, special state censuses of veterans, and territorial censuses are also available. Some states had regular censuses taken between the federal censuses, particularly in the 19th century. Some of these state censuses give more information than the federal census; you should check both censuses. Sometimes state censuses were taken for special purposes, such as the 1906–07 census of Confederate veterans in Alabama.

If your ancestors ever lived in an area under territorial status, you will find the territorial censuses important.

These may be published in the series of Territorial Papers; a complete set of the printed edition (selected papers) is in many good libraries, and a microfilm edition (complete papers) is in some major libraries.

For particulars, see *State Censuses,* by Henry J. Dubester; the first edition was published by the government in 1948. For other particulars, refer to a genealogical handbook or related publications. Library card catalogs will have *subject* entries under these headings: County, State, or Country— Census; *main* entries will be listed under the government agency issuing the publication—for example, *U.S. Bureau of Census—Census* (by number and year). Be careful to check the special card catalogs and inventories in the research departments; many libraries catalog their microfilm and other nonbook material this way, rather than in regular card catalogs.

Extracting the Census Data

Indicate the machine-numbered page on which the data appear in the census rather than a handwritten page number. The machine numbers will clarify the instructions when you request copies, and they will conform to genealogical usage.

Extracts from censuses are easily obtained by using printed forms specially designed to conform to the *columnar arrangement* of each census. These forms are included in the *Logbook.* Be sure to extract all of the information contained in each census record that is related in any way to your families. Many genealogists advise making extracts for all families of the same name(s), because later research will probably reveal connections between your families and those unknown to you in the beginning.

EXTRACT FROM 1880 CENSUS

State __PA__ County or Parish __Luzerne__ Township, Ward or Beat _____ Date of Enumeration _____ Sup. Dist. No. _____ Enum. Dist. No. _____

Index compiled by _____ Extract by _____ Publication No. _____ Reel No. _____

Page	Dwelling No.	Family No.	Names	Color	Sex	Age prior to June 1st	Month of birth if born in census year	Relationship to head of house	Single	Married	Widowed/Divorced	Married in census year	Occupation	Miscellaneous	Cannot read	Cannot write	Place of birth	Place of birth of mother	Place of birth of father
			Jeffries, Richard R.			51												Wales		
			Hannah			46		Wife									Wales		
			Martha			23		Daug.									Wales		
			Winnifred			17		Daug.									Wales		
			Matilda			15		Daug.									Wales		
			Mary A.			13		Daug.									PA		
			Ruth			9		Daug.									PA		
			Thomas			7		Son									PA		
			William B.			5		Son									PA		

(Perhaps our Gwendolyn could have been the second child (between the 23 yr. old and the 17 yr. old, and have married by this time 1880?). Estate papers of Richard R. Jeffries, Luzerne Co., 1907, number 178, reveal the confirmation of the hypothesis. Papers photocopied 22 May 1970.)

Form 12

Analyzing the Census Data

You should carefully analyze the information obtained from the census in order to draw tentative conclusions and support or disprove them by more research. You will learn many facts about your families from the 1900 census. Even the 1880 census may enable you to approximate the date of a marriage where marriage records are unavailable. *My wife's grandmother, Gwendolyn, does not appear in the 1880 census under the Jeffries' household. In trying to ascertain the date of her marriage, the facts revealed that her husband Herbert Mathewson, was not 18 until 1878. Therefore, it is highly probable that they married between 1878 and 1880.*

Often, you have to try to link facts that you have gathered. *Edward Brobst (my wife's grandfather) appears in the 1880 census of Plymouth, Luzerne, Co. PA, as a stabel [sic] boss. His age at the time coincided with information about an Edward in the 1870 census of Salem Township, which was 25 miles from Plymouth. Correlation of these links eventually revealed that all the information pertained to the same person, my wife's grandfather, Edward Brobst.*

Since adequate tracing of your ancestry depends upon developing many different types of evidence for links between persons, it is important to gather substantial data relating to each family member. Clues must be gleaned from every possible source, and these should be pursued by intensive research.

Abstracting Requires Background Knowledge

In order to use estate records, you should follow these suggestions. First, find out where your ancestor's estate settlement or his transfer of land ownership was recorded. In the South the State Archives usually maintains the older county records. However, Alabama and Mississippi are exceptions.

Published inventories of these records may be available, but the inventories may be out of date (for example, the inventories issued during the Works Projects Administration era). Some inventories have appeared occasionally in genealogical journals and may be cited in the *Genealogical Periodical Annual Index*. Others may be available in historical library collections and in state archives.

Studying the history of the court system of your ancestor's state will prove valuable. A more complete discussion of this subject may be found in articles on genealogical research in the specific state, or in publications from the state archives. Competent local genealogists may be able to advise you, and they often know details about matters that have not been publicized. You may wish to consult the state archivist, the state's major research librarians, the county clerk, and a scholar well versed in the state's legal history.

It is costly to obtain photocopies of all documents, such as wills and deeds, but they will eliminate return visits, and you

will be able to review them for legal terminology and procedure.

It is important to understand the meaning of legal terms
you encounter in the records. You also need to understand
the legal history of the state. If you do not understand the
procedures and terminology referred to, you will miss important information and will not comprehend the meaning
of some action or record.

A few examples will illustrate the meaning of common
legal terminology:

Et uxor (now usually *et ux*). Latin term meaning "and wife."

Fee simple (often just *fee*). The owner is entitled to the
entire property with unconditional power during his life
and descending to his heirs upon his death without a will.

Infant. Referring to a minor, not of full legal age.

Relict. The one who survives of a married pair, husband or
wife.

An extensive reading of the documents may develop a
knowledge and familiarity with the terminology. Try to
consult an old law dictionary of the period which you are
researching, and you will be rewarded by learning the
meaning of the words used at that time. Compare the older
definition of your terminology with the current *Black's Law
Dictionary,* published by West Publishing Company. Val D.
Greenwood's *Researcher's Guide to American Genealogy*
(Genealogical Publishing Co., 1973) has a helpful selection
of legal definitions.

Making the Abstract

The abstract can be made on a standard 8½" x 11" sheet of
paper, or a 4" x 6" file card or other form. The heading of
the abstract should show (for your convenience) three elements: (1) name of person whose record is abstracted, (2)

county (and parish if appropriate) of record, (3) date of document (not date of recording).

Then give the abstract in this order (varying with the type of record being abstracted):

† Title of the volume, including name of county or juris-
diction
† The volume letter or number
† The inclusive dates of the volume
† The page number
† The type of document abstracted
† Name of person who created the document. If references are made to his residence, occupation, age, or
health (even inferential), these should be noted.
† Date of death (if given)
† Date of recording
† In abstracting, always use the pronouns used in the
document itself to avoid confusion (for example, to my
son John, to my brother George). Always use the exact
order given in the document. List the essentials of each
bequest, including land description, amounts of money
(including kind of money), all identifiable property
specified, and names of Negro slaves (if any).
† Miscellaneous details, such as explanations of bequests,
restrictions or special privileges, should be abstracted.
† List the name(s) of the executor(s), and record any
relationship with the author (or other detail about the
executor) that is given in the document.
† Specify the names of the witnesses.
† Conclude with an indication of the signature of the
author of the document. If he made his mark instead of
writing his signature, this should be indicated. (His
mark may differentiate him from others of the same
name.)

If the document is a deed, the grantor(s) and the gran-
tee(s) should be named. The places of residence (including

the parishes) of the parties should be stated (generally a most valuable piece of genealogical evidence) as well as the price that was paid and any terms specified.

A precise description of the land, including the acreage and the location, should be given.

Miscellaneous details should be abstracted, such as relationships, special terms, and restrictions or special privileges.

Specify the names of witnesses and the signature(s) of the grantor(s) (or indicate if the grantor made his mark instead).

Conclude with the acknowledgement—check to see if the deed was acknowledged by the grantor personally in open court. This frequently is of special value for genealogical purposes, particularly due to the number and extent of migrations.

Be sure to include the release of dower by the grantor's wife. This is frequently a separate record. This was usually required in most southern states. If the wife died prior to the transfer of the property, of course there could be no release of dower.

The absence of a record of release of dower does not prove that the wife predeceased the husband. Release of dower sometimes is recorded much later in the court records than the original transaction of property transfer. Children may later quitclaim the property so that it can be sold, and this occasionally provides genealogical evidence of the mother's name and other relationships.

Published Abstracts

There is much danger in relying upon published and unpublished typed abstracts of records. The abstractor may miscopy the name Robertson for Roberson. He may mistype the name Swingel for Swingle by transposing letters.

He may omit a child or a witness. He may assume a spelling rather than copy the exact spelling. He may not index his records thoroughly. He may omit the description of the land (thus omitting valuable clues regarding ancestry). He may neglect to name specific items which may be of value in tracing the ancestry. He is not legally bound to abstract the record correctly.

The fact that there are notable exceptions abstracted by skilled genealogical researchers serves to prove that published or typed abstracts done by others are seldom reliable for completeness and accuracy. The exceptions of note include those by John Frederick Dorman, Caroline T. Moore, and Alexander M. Walker.

Abstract volumes usually include a valuable index supplied by the compiler. It includes the witnesses, which do not appear in court indexes. Furthermore, abstract volumes may cover a greater chronological range of records within a volume than a court index. The deeds may not be recorded until many years after the property was transferred. These may be found in the abstract volume. Some abstracts may include complementary matter supplied by the compiler, and this can prove helpful.

Generally, you should not rely on compiled abstracts, but they may be useful to supply clues to research the original records.

Wills and Administrations

You should continue to accumulate all relevant records from official sources to develop an accurate base from which to trace your ancestry. Your ancestors' records provide valuable and authentic details, especially those that were kept for legal purposes. Estate records, in most instances, will indicate the relationship between the person making the will (testator) and the person receiving the property. Usually, you will find each child mentioned. His relationship to the testator may be indicated along with the distribution of the property. Occasionally, grandchildren, nieces, nephews, brothers, sisters, parents, and some non-relatives are named. Sometimes, of course, a person may be omitted from the will deliberately. You may discover an explanation for this, such as a prior transfer of property to that individual or the death of a child before the estate was settled.

Wills can be very useful genealogically. *My wife's Welsh great-grandfather mentioned every living child in his will. He stated the married names of the wedded daughters, as is customary. This gave us evidence to confirm a surmise of ours, that his daughter Gwendolyn had married Herbert Mathewson. He mentioned a stepdaughter of whom we did not know. He also mentioned the children of a deceased daughter, and this helped us to narrow the search for a record of her death. All of this and more came from a one-page document, which we copied from the courthouse record.*

The law requires that wills be proven in court, and other documents are added to the total record during the process of estate settlement. *In the probate file, we found signed receipts for payments made to fulfill the conditions of the will, and these supplied us with signatures of the living children and orphaned grandchildren. Another record was the first and final account (there are usually several accounts) of the testator's very small estate. This account gave us a helpful insight into our Welsh family's circumstances in 1907.*

Thus, as you search back for the probate records of your ancestors, the family will come alive for you, and you will obtain helpful information. Sometimes you will be disappointed because you cannot find the probate record of an ancestor. Not everyone's estate went through probate. Not all wills were recorded even if they were probated. We haven't been able to locate any probate records of my wife's Mathewson ancestors. It is possible that some may be found in other counties, because wills are required to be filed and probate of the estates handled in the county where the person resided at death. No doubt you will encounter similar problems, but you will learn to work around them.

The application (petition) for probate may contain a list of possible heirs, their relationship to the deceased, and their addresses (even if they are not named in the will).

The executor is required to report to the court about his transactions with the estate. He is also required to inventory and appraise the estate's property. Sometimes the deceased's property is sold at public auction. Perhaps you can remember when a family member's farm tools, implements, livestock, household goods, and farm were sold by public auction. The records of such appraisals and auctions are useful for your family history.

Administrations

When a person dies without leaving a will, he is said to be intestate. His estate must go through a probate proceeding according to the laws of the state of his last residence. This proceeding is commonly called the administration of an estate. The court appoints a person to administer the distribution of the estate. The administrator must follow the law and provide specified reports to the court until a final settlement is arranged. The letters of administration are usually granted to the surviving spouse or the next-of-kin. If there is no surviving spouse, the court usually selects the most qualified from the next-of-kin. Generally the court follows guidelines, which may help you find a clue of genealogical value (residents are preferred to nonresidents and whole-blood relatives are preferred to half-blood relatives).

In most states there must be assets sufficient to justify granting letters of administration. This may account for the lack of probate records of some of our ancestors. However, these records may be so useful that a diligent search is required. The administrator must account in writing to the court, and his records must show how the estate is divided. Specific family information should appear since each legal heir's name must be contained in documents filed with the court. Sometimes the documents include proof of relationship.

The probate office maintains the records of bonds for those who administered estates, usually showing family relationships. Men administered estates for their wives and for their close relatives.

The cost paid to record a will is recorded in fee books. They usually give the date of recording and supply some data as a substitute source for missing wills and administrations. Order books record the court orders, which may be searched to supply additional information or clues.

Guardianship records may exist on your ancestors. If the ancestor was survived by minor children, a guardian had to be appointed to manage their properties and to be responsible for them. Legacies from grandparents or other relatives resulted in guardianships. Guardianships are called "tutorships" in Louisiana.

You may learn your ancestor's age from guardianship proceedings and records. Apprenticeship papers were often included in guardianship records.

Trip to Courthouse

Now, it's time for your trip to the courthouse. You should take along a supply of coins, because many of the copying machines are coin-operated; the copying fees are more expensive than those in libraries. The documents will be useful to compare with earlier records as your family history develops.

You should remember that while the county probate court and its staff are public servants, their primary obligation is to maintain the records. Generally, you will find the staff quite occupied with the daily work load. When you ask for help, be businesslike but cordial. Ask for specific directions about using and locating the records.

My visits have brought gratifying results. When I have asked for help in uncertain situations, my inquiries have never been rebuffed. Because the older staff members are very familiar with the records, you should ask them for help at an early stage of your research. Occasionally, you may find a person who is very knowledgeable about the county and its families.

The minutes contain only the barest record of court actions. Many primary documents that are submitted to the court as evidence may be filed in case files. They are usually given a number that is recorded in the minutes or record of the court. Case files were used a great deal in courthouses and lawyer's offices, and are still in use in some locations. They are generally contained in metal or wooden drawers to accommodate legal size (8½" by 14") documents, which are folded into four panels.

These primary estate documents are important to your research, and you must search diligently for them. Sometimes they will be referred to in the court transactions and recordings, but they will not always be in or with the main record. You should learn how to identify and search for those primary documents (petition for probate, original will, petition for letters of administration, letters testamentary and inventories). Many of them contain valuable family information beyond the required data for the estate settlement. We noted earlier that they may contain the signatures of some of your ancestors and/or relatives.

My youngest daughter and I searched in the subbasement of a courthouse for similar records a few years ago. These primary records were supposed to be in a case file of old records of the 19th century, and were of no current judicial interest. Therefore, they had been relegated to a sizeable mass of records in the subbasement for storage. They were not in the appropriate file drawer. But we found a jumbled drawer labeled X-Y-Z, which contained the valuable Bilheimer family records. About two years later, a catastrophic flood in that county completely ruined all of the material in the subbasement. Emergency health requirements necessitated burial of the sodden mass of documents. Luckily, we had obtained complete copies on our first visit of everything in the Bilheimer family file.

Such primary documents provide important evidence for your family history. We gleaned from the Bilheimer family file the complete list of the great-grandmother's siblings, the extent of the estate, the other county in which the family resided (we already knew of one), and many other useful facts.

The courts with jurisdiction over probate matters are known by different names in different regions and states. These courts are known as Probate Court in many southern states, as Ordinary Court in Georgia, Surrogate Court in New York and New Jersey, and Orphans' Court in Pennsylvania. Cities such as Philadelphia and Baltimore, and some states, have Registers of Wills. To determine the exact terminology for the court, consult Noel C. Stevenson's *Search and Research* (Revised edition, 1973).

Court Indexes

You may be surprised when you first examine the courthouse indexes. Someone has suggested that these index systems were created by madmen, or by lawyers determined to thwart the public use of records. The indexes were actually designed to expedite the use of records by the court's staff. A system is needed to tie together information related to people who have similar names that are spelled differently.

Thus my wife's maternal family, Mathewson, is indexed with those of Matteson and Mathison, and her Sutliff references are indexed with those of Sutcliff and Setliff. As you search these indexes, the association of similar names should be noted; in earlier generations, spellings of names were not as standardized as they tend to be now. Studying other types of surname variations may be beneficial.

Among these indexes are some which seem to be exasperating. They may be of value to the court, but they are disconcerting to one who does not use them regularly.

The Campbell Index system indexes names alphabetically only by the initials of the surname and the given name. Thus, the names of James Scarborough, John Sutliff, and Jasper Stewart would be indexed on the same page in the order of recording.

The Russell Index system arranges surnames by key letters *within* the name. Thus, under the key letter *L,* the index would list any name with the letter *L* within it with all names with the same initial letter, such as *C.* Thus, Cole, Clower, and Cullison would be indexed on the same index page.

The Cott Indexes are varied, and they are planned so that record books are economically used and the clerk's time is more efficiently utilized. These indexes generally disperse surnames with like initials by means of the given names with like initials. Thus, all surnames with initials D, E, F, G, H would be entered on a specified numbered page if their *given* names began with the initial letter R.

There are other index systems used in courthouses; you may have to familiarize yourself with them. They will sometimes test your powers of observation and concentration and steal precious time from research. You should become acquainted with the particular system before you use it. If you do not understand the system, your search may end fruitlessly.

There is an excellent discussion of these indexes by Morris L. Radoff in *The County Courthouses and Records of Maryland Part Two: The Records* (1963) also reproduced in *Genealogy,* a publication of the Genealogy Section, Indiana Historical Society, by Willard Heiss, November 1974.

Other Probate Records

Besides the estate records, there are a few other types of records in probate or similar courts that you should remember and use. There may be petitions for the court to rule on specific estate matters. These will name the deceased person, the date of probate of the estate, the date of the petition, the residence of the decedent and the heirs (if known), the names of the heirs, their ages, and their relationships to the decedent.

Remember that a kindly inquiry of an elderly staff member may divulge the existence and location of a record or group of records not usually found in probate offices. It is worth your time to wait and talk with this individual, and then to examine the record if one is found.

Local Land Records

There is another extensive class of local records that pertains to land: it includes deeds and mortgages. Since many of our ancestors owned land, you can appreciate the importance of these records.

Land records usually reveal the date of deed, the date of recording (sometimes recorded years after the purchase), the grantee's (purchaser's) name in full legal form, his county or place of residence, and a statement of the location and measurements of the land. These records normally contain signatures of witnesses. When land is transferred between relatives, family relationships are frequently indicated. A wife's given name appears in records of land transfers in many states.

Your ancestors' purchases of land may be recorded with the Recorder of Deeds at the appropriate county court office. In Connecticut, Rhode Island, and Vermont, land purchases are found in the town records. Many deeds (and wills) have not been recorded. In some states, early land records have been put on microfilm, and copies have been placed in the state archives. You will find the current information regarding the records of a specific state summarized in the latest editions of genealogical manuals; you may also direct inquiries to the respective state archives.

Mortgages frequently accompany land purchases, and often contain information which supplements the deed record. In searching mortgage records for information on your ancestors, you will find facts about them that will aid your research. Mortgage records sometimes indicate the transfer of land, which may not be noted in the deed records. Sometimes mortgages reflect family relationships not found in other records.

For example, a careful reading of the mortgage records in Luzerne County, Pennsylvania, clarified the distinction between two Edward Brobsts; one was my wife's grandfather, and the other appeared to be related collaterally—not in the direct line of ancestry. Since they had property transactions in the same town during the same period, confusion about the identity of the two had to be resolved before we could safely proceed with our research.

Your ancestor may be mentioned in a mortgage record even if he is not mentioned in the deed records, especially if he acquired land earlier by gift, or inheritance, or if he transacted much business on credit in the twentieth century.

Another good point to remember is that mortgage indexes can help you find the given names of possible relatives; other records may be inadequate, such as censuses before 1850. Land records are indexed according to the full name of a family member. Then the mortgage indexes may help, because all entries of the same surname are indexed together. Also, mortgage indexes usually list the township or location of your ancestor's land. There are two deed indexes: grantor (seller) and grantee (purchaser), and in some states a cross index includes both.

Intestate administrations required the family to quiet title of land which the deceased owned before it could be sold. Thus, the deceased's heirs had to release their legal claims to the land. The releases signed by the heir(s) often included the signatures of the spouses of sons and daughters to transfer title. Thereby you may obtain the full names of the in-laws. Places of residences of the heirs are sometimes mentioned in such records. Thus, genealogical information is found in deed records.

Even when property is conveyed normally, the relationship between grantor and grantee is usually stated. And grantors often mention that the tract was conveyed to the wife from the estate of her father and may give his name, thus identifying the wife's maiden name and father.

The variety of land-related records suggests that you should examine leases, contracts, judgments, liens, and other documents pertaining to the property or the family name. *Information on my wife's Brobst ancestry is found in various records in Columbia County, Pennsylvania. Her ancestors are listed in the grantor index, which includes a variety of records: assignment, release, bond, oath, and power of attorney.* In many cases the legal agent's name is indexed rather than the grantor's name.

Bills of sale involving transfer of slaves were frequently recorded in deed books, especially in the South.

When original land entries are being researched, you may find applications, warrants, and patents for the land. Application was filed first, stating the person's residence and other details. A warrant was issued granting the right to a specific amount of land. Then a survey was made to determine the boundaries; the survey included a map of the property. A patent was issued which constituted a deed for the property. This pattern was generally followed both under the colonial and federal governments. Some states required the warrantee to list his native country.

Property Identification Surveys and Maps

In most of the country, land was acquired and described in terms of a rectangular survey of the territory. Land in the expansion states was usually mapped and disposed of through the rectangular survey system. The expansion states were those first settled after the original thirteen states. The Federal Government adopted this system in 1785. After improvements were made, the system continued to the present time. In the older states, it is more difficult to describe and to locate property sites, and considerable litigation arose concerning boundaries.

Under the rectangular survey, from a chosen point where the latitude and longitude were known, a line was drawn north and south to make the principal meridian. A line was drawn east and west to make the base line. Sometimes the base line was established at a different point on the principal meridian. It was established at a previously known latitude; for example, the boundary line between Tennessee and Alabama.

Townships were laid out with boundaries running north and south and east and west. The township was 6 miles on each of the four sides, making 36 square miles. You can count the number of townships north or south from the base line, such as township north. Then count the number of townships (called ranges to distinguish the direction) east or west of the principal meridian, such as range five west. A shorthand is used: T7N and R5W. The name of the principal meridian is mentioned; for example, the Huntsville (Alabama) Meridian.

Townships are subdivided into 36 one-mile square sections, and the sections may be quartered into four equal units of 160 acres; these may be quartered again into 40-acre divisions. Further divisions are common in more populous areas.

The 36 sections in a township are numbered in sequence; they begin in the northeast corner and proceed westward to the end of the township. The next row of sections runs eastward, and then this process is repeated. Sections consist of 640 acres; therefore, smaller holdings are described in terms of quarters, such as "southwest quarter" (SW ¼).

Thus, you will likely encounter descriptions as follows: NW¼ of SW ¼ of Sec. 12 T 7 N, R 5 W. You can locate any property within the rectangular survey with this system. In the courthouse and at each Secretary of State's office, you will find the tract book which lists the grants of property by section in each township of the county, giving the original grantee's names and patent numbers.

Since the vast bulk of our land is identified by this system, you will need to understand it. Then, when you go to the courthouse to examine records of land transactions for your research, you will understand them.

Land in the older eastern states is described in the records by terms commonly used in the native country. Thus we find terms such as furlongs, chains, perches (poles or rods), and links. There are 25 links to a rod, 100 links to a chain, and 10 chains to a furlong.

Land was usually not transferred in squares (or sections) as it was in the later public domain states. Townships were laid out quite differently in the eastern and southern states. In New England, townships were called towns. Title records are quite different in these regions. Also, Kentucky and Tennessee have records which are similar to those of their parent states, Virginia and North Carolina respectively. Much of the land in Florida, Alabama, Mississippi, and Louisiana was granted by foreign governments before they were public domain states. Thus, grants were made under those governments which do not match the rectangular survey process, nor the terminology of description prevailing in the English colonies. You must be familiar with the appropriate terms of description when you are working in those regions.

Maps and Their Importance

You should become familiar with the plats and maps of your research areas; you will need to understand common road maps, land ownership maps, and maps that were drawn up during a particular era. Maps which indicate the topography of the area are particularly useful, since they reveal the natural barriers to travel such as mountains.

Mountains were major barriers to travel and migration, whereas waterways were common transportation routes. Your ancestors may have traveled a waterway to market or to attend church or school. Therefore, in seeking church and school records for earlier times, a careful study of the maps will aid you in determining the possible sources for records. In our times, man's technological capability to build roads across and through mountains has changed transportation and migration patterns significantly.

The land ownership maps are particularly interesting and useful. They are based on land ownership at the time the maps were drafted. A considerable number of these maps are available in research libraries and may be purchased from the Photoduplication Service of the Library of Congress. Other government agencies, such as the National Archives and the Coast and Geodetic Survey, have maps available for sale. There are numerous local maps of towns, counties, and states that may be found at various institutions. Also historical societies and agencies, collectors, local historians, and genealogical enthusiasts will have access to maps.

Scan these maps for a view of family sites, godparents' homes, neighbors' homes, friends' homes, churches, mills, stores, schools, and depots. The plat books in the county courthouse also provide visual clues for the family history.

You should acquire copies of maps pertinent to the locales

and times in which your ancestors lived. A sequence of maps of the county will be helpful in studying the development of the area and your family's relationship to the development.

Abstracts of Records Relating to Land

Private abstract offices and title companies were established to arrange abstracts of official land records. All entries relating to real property are maintained according to location. All actions regarding a specific piece of land are assembled to determine the right of the seller to dispose of the land free of encumbrances. These companies abstract courthouse records relating to the property, not only deeds and mortgages, but also wills, administrations, and other types of records. These records are obviously useful for your genealogical purposes.

Abstracts, though expensive, may provide valuable information, which would justify their costs. Additional data or information may be obtained and examined from the original courthouse records. When courthouse records are missing or have been destroyed, data may be found in abstract offices. Since they are not public records but are the product of private companies, fees must usually be paid for the use of this information.

Tax Records

Gaps in your data regarding family members can often be filled to some extent by tax records. Since these records are based on annual taxes, they can supply clues to an ancestor's arrival and departure from a specific area. The extent and value of their landholdings and personal property can provide evidence of their financial condition. Personal property tax lists record a more comprehensive coverage than real property tax lists. However, they are limited to the head of the household. Study of these lists may provide significant clues.

Church and Cemetery Records

You will need to gather information from church and cemetery records, since they are related to official birth and death records. We have waited until now to discuss the church and cemetery records, because the probate records (wills and estates) and the local land records (deeds and mortgages) are generally a better class of evidence. Probate and land records have legal value.

You will learn, to your dismay, that most church records are not indexed; this increases the difficulty of using them. You will discover that church records of many faiths do not provide explicit birth or death information.

Accuracy and completeness of church records depend on the diligence of the record keeper, whether he is the minister, the clerk, or other church official. Public record keeping is supervised by an official who is obligated to do so. But you may find carelessly kept public records or well-kept church records.

Church records are generally of such potential value that you should understand how to use them. In the absence of direct entries, search by date, era, or names of related persons or siblings to obtain information.

You may find a baptismal (christening) record near the birth date; the parents and sponsors (often called godparents) may also be named. The sponsors' names are generally useful for further genealogical search, since they may be relatives or neighbors. Funeral and other death records may bear the date of the funeral rather than the death date.

If you descend from families who were members of the Episcopal church, you will generally find that they kept meticulous church records. The Presbyterian church has a centralized archive. Records of Quakers, Moravians, or Lutherans may give you much genealogical information. The Quakers recorded births, marriages, transfer of members from their meetings (congregations), and the disciplinary action taken against members for various causes (particularly for marrying non-Quakers). Moravians in Pennsylvania and North Carolina have excellent records, which are similar in content to the Quaker records. The Moravian records of North Carolina were edited by Adelaide L. Fries and published. Records of defunct Lutheran churches have been gathered together in regional archives, but you must be able to read the difficult German script, or get someone to do so. Catholic records are seldom accessible; it may be difficult to get information from their respositories.

If you are one of the multitude who has Baptist or Methodist antecedents, your problems of research are compounded. Baptist records are congregationally owned. In recent decades, some of these records have been deposited or microfilmed in Baptist historical libraries in each of the southern states or in somewhat comprehensive regional centers at Nashville and Rochester, New York.

Baptist records are not easily located and usually lack the birth, death, and marriage records. If you study the membership rolls carefully, and read the quarterly or monthly church conference minutes meticulously, you may find the date your ancestor joined the church. Occasionally you may discover the name of a church that your ancestor attended previously. Marriage records *per se* are not in Baptist records, but sometimes the data may be recorded in a minister's diary.

Also, Methodist records are gradually being gathered into regional centers at seminaries and historical libraries. Methodist records, too, lack vital records, although christenings may be recorded, and marriages may be entered voluntarily in the record by the minister. First, try to get access to church records through the pastor, clerk, or other officers of the church. They may have the records or know of their location. Next, you should contact the local historical society or local library. Then try the state denominational library, the state archival agency, or the regional depository of denominational records. Since the Mormons have been microfilming church and other records assiduously, there is a possibility that the records may be on film at the state archives, a local cooperating agency, or the Genealogical Society Library in Salt Lake City. You will find appropriate reference works regarding church records in the larger libraries.

Cemetery Records and Gravestone Inscriptions

Cemetery records and gravestone inscriptions usually record date of death (not always accurate), date of birth (less dependable), or age in years, months, and days (again not fully dependable). Remember that cemetery records in the custodian's (sexton's) office may be more complete and accurate than the gravestone inscriptions. These records should give the name of the family member who purchased the plot, and they may record the relationships of the persons buried in the plot. Also, the name of the present owner may give you more information. You should offer to pay for any copies of records that you obtain. Many times the gravestone inscriptions will include the marriage status. Since stonecutters make mistakes, use dates that appear on the inscriptions cautiously. Lack of funds frequently delayed purchase of gravestone markers; consequently, information sometimes was given from memory rather than from written records. Family relationships are often given on the stones and sometimes you may find other facts about the career or character of the deceased on them. Gravestone inscriptions are often called tombstone or monumental inscriptions.

Copied or compiled material from libraries is very helpful but it must be verified by actual examination of the tombstone itself. Enthusiasts in local history and genealogy have assembled massive amounts of transcripts of gravestone inscriptions in the geographic areas of their interest. These copies, usually typed, have been placed in libraries, historical societies, archives, and manuscript collections. Hereditary societies, such as the Daughters of the American Revolution and the Colonial Dames, have been particularly diligent and beneficial in this work. Genealogical periodicals and some historical journals have published inscriptions. If you are able to find the transcripts of gravestone inscriptions for cemeteries where you have ancestors buried, you will be grateful to those who compiled the information.

Some county inventories of cemetery inscriptions have been published (for example, Pike County, Alabama). Be cautious and verify the data by visiting the actual site of the grave, if possible. You may be amused at the subtle humor or versifying on some of the tombstones. Several books have been published that reveal the humor in a somber subject.

Newspaper Obituaries and Other Vital Records

You may have found obituaries of deceased family members among clippings in family papers or scrapbooks. Therefore, you know that newspapers are valuable sources of family information. These obituaries usually give not only the name but also the date and place of death and burial, age or date of birth, residence in recent past, brief biography, and names of survivors and their relationships to the deceased. However, newspaper obituaries are only as reliable as the person who gave the information.

Examine these obituaries for any discrepancies in the data. *Great-aunt Mabel was reported in an obituary to have been born in Yatesville, while family information had reported her to be born in West Pittston, which was across the river and several miles away. The obituary gave an incorrect year of birth, an incorrect first name for her father, and an incorrect spelling of her mother's first name. However, this obituary provided some accurate information, which aided us significantly in our family search.*

An obituary may state a fact that will lead to other sources of information. Such details may include membership in a fraternal order, affiliation with a specific church, date and place of marriage, cause of death, and locations of relatives. The information for the death certificate may have been supplied by a different person than the informant for the newspaper account. You then have two sources and versions of the particulars which should be examined and compared.

I worked as a reporter for a morning newspaper that tried to be a reliable recorder of every birth, marriage, and death in the county. But the afternoon papers tended to record primarily what was submitted to them; thus, they were more selective and more erroneous. Remember that an examination of more than one newspaper in the locale is advisable. Competing newspapers do not print the same selections of details. Search for the fullest and most accurate newspaper account.

Marriages (and anniversaries) reported in newspapers customarily include the date and place of marriage, residences, occupations, and names of parents. Church affiliations will usually be mentioned.

Divorces may be reported in newspapers, but more complete and useful data will appear in the government records.

You will find official record of the distribution of property, names and ages of children, as well as the date of marriage.

The newspapers may be readily accessible if you are in the publication locale. The courthouse, the newspaper office, and the public library may be likely places to find volumes. You should also try the state archives or a well-established library. If you can't locate the newspapers in any of these places, what should you do?

You can find several aids to newspaper use at nearly all prominent libraries. Even some of the modest-size libraries have excellent research facilities. You will find newspaper bibliographies essential to your research. Winifred Gregory, *American Newspapers, 1821–1936: A Union List of Files Available in the U.S. and Canada* is now woefully out of date, and reports holdings, especially of courthouses which no longer exist or have been transferred to other facilities. For the period up to 1820, a splendid resource is Clarence S. Brigham's *History and Bibliography of American Newspapers, 1690–1820,* with supplements. Specialized state bibliographies are sometimes available; they provide more detailed listings and holdings, and you should consult these. They are found under *American Newspapers—(state)* in the subject catalogs of libraries.

Since so much microfilming has been done, it is important to check the latest edition of *Newspapers in Microform; United States, 1948–1972;* it is issued by the Library of Congress. State and local lists may be of value to you, because much of the microfilming is not reported to the national center. They are found under *Newspapers in Microform—Bibliography* in the subject catalogs. Once you find a newspaper available on microfilm, your library may borrow the appropriate reels on inter-library loan.

Don't get bogged down with the charming and sometimes quaint advertising and news items. Concentrate on your research first. When you have done your research, then treat yourself to leisure reading.

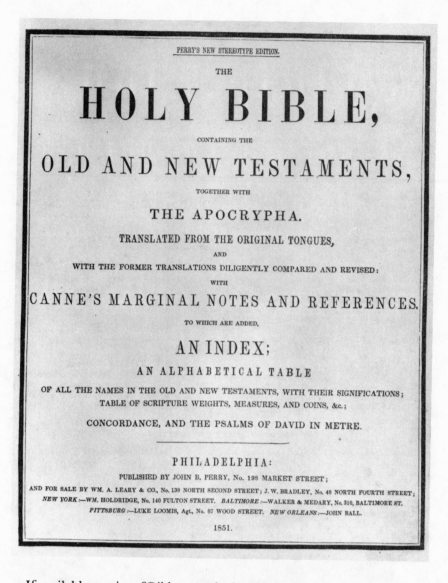

PERRY'S NEW STEREOTYPE EDITION.

THE

HOLY BIBLE,

CONTAINING THE

OLD AND NEW TESTAMENTS,

TOGETHER WITH

THE APOCRYPHA.

TRANSLATED FROM THE ORIGINAL TONGUES,

AND

WITH THE FORMER TRANSLATIONS DILIGENTLY COMPARED AND REVISED:

WITH

CANNE'S MARGINAL NOTES AND REFERENCES.

TO WHICH ARE ADDED,

AN INDEX;

AN ALPHABETICAL TABLE

OF ALL THE NAMES IN THE OLD AND NEW TESTAMENTS, WITH THEIR SIGNIFICATIONS;
TABLE OF SCRIPTURE WEIGHTS, MEASURES, AND COINS, &c.;

CONCORDANCE, AND THE PSALMS OF DAVID IN METRE.

PHILADELPHIA:

PUBLISHED BY JOHN B. PERRY, No. 198 MARKET STREET;

AND FOR SALE BY WM. A. LEARY & CO., No. 138 NORTH SECOND STREET; J. W. BRADLEY, No. 48 NORTH FOURTH STREET; NEW YORK:—WM. HOLDRIDGE, No. 140 FULTON STREET. BALTIMORE:—WALKER & MEDARY, No. 310, BALTIMORE ST. PITTSBURG:—LUKE LOOMIS, Agt., No. 87 WOOD STREET, NEW ORLEANS:—JOHN BALL.

1851.

If available, copies of Bible records should always include a photocopy of the title page or the New Testament title page. If the date is not included on the title page, you need a copy of the copyright page (verso) containing the copyright notice, publisher's code, or similar identification.

Bible records are valuable evidence if they appear to be contemporary with the events. However, this record indicates that all the entries were probably made (or copied) at one time—after the last birth on 15 Sep 1892. They may have been copied from an earlier record or from memory.

Postcards can reveal important information. This one mentions Evelyn (sister-in-law), Molly (sister), Cousin Em (hospitalized), Frank S. (visitor or relative), and Nancy (preparing for wedding).

A treasure for a genealogist to behold is a family album, a scrap-book, or even a box of pictures. Undated scrapbooks and uniden-tified photographs can be used to jog relatives' memories.

The taped interview is a valuable tool in your genealogical research. These are usually very interesting interviews which reveal
the personalities of your ancestors, not just the data.

Your research is greatly aided by adequate facilities and helpful
librarians as found in this special collection department of a library.

Files of notes and forms may be kept in storage boxes and file folders. However, you may wish to keep your family histories in loose-leaf binders; if you use forms with punched holes (as in the *Logbook*), it is easy to add to them.

Annals of, vols. 1-2, by Caroline P. Wilson
(1928, 1933, repr 1969) bk rev   TAN 16:4:153
Early Baptists, biog sketches, names S1-V
GPGM 6:1:25 6:2:93 6:3:151 6:4:201
D.A.R. Bible Records, 2nd ser., vol. 1, index
GGSQ 5:2:125
Cherokee Indian Agency, baptismal register,
April 1805   GGSQ 5:3:225
List of claimants, damages by Creek Indians,
1822   GG 1:2:-
List of dissenters to the Revolution, 1774
GG 1:2:-
1840 census index, by Woods & Sheffield (1969)
book review   SGE 10:51:3
Greensborough Methodist Church Circuit, mem-
bership roll, 1836   GG 1:1:-
Hist Collections, Ga. Chapters, DAR, 4 vols.
(repr 1968) book review   TVG 13:1:40
GH 23:1:53 23:3:298 TAN 16:3:106 16:4:153
Land lottery, 1807, by Silas E. Lucas (repr
1968) bk review
GH 23:2:97 TAN 16:3:106 TVG 13:2:91
1832 (Cherokee), by James F. Smith (1838,
repr 1968) bk review
GH 23:3:296 TAN 16:3:106 TVG 13:2:91
marriage records, 1782-1795   GG 1:1:- 1:2:-
marr & death recs from newspaper 1763-1820, by
by Mary B. Warren (c1968) bk rev   GH 23:1:2
marr & death recs from Savannah newspaper,
1819-20   GGM 31:2115
marr recs from Milledgeville newspapers, 1859-
1860   GGM 32:2225
muster rolls [various] 1775-94   GGM 32:2213
Revolutionary pensioners, list, 1820 GG 1:1:-
Rev. soldiers, roster, 2 vols, by Mrs. Howard
H. McCall (repr 1968) bh review
GGSQ 5:2:177 GH 23:4:445
by Lucian L. Knight (1920, repr 1967) bk rev
GGSQ 5:2:177
GERALDINES of Allen, Ireland, gen   IreG 4:2:93
GERMANNA recs, no. 11 [Carpenter & Wayland gens]
(1968) book review   TVG 13:1:37
GERMANY, Plittersdorf, St. Evergislus Church cem

Articles pertaining to the state, county, type of records, or methodology of genealogical procedures, as well as to a specific family, are identified in the *Genealogical Periodical Annual Index*. Abbreviations of periodicals are explained in each volume of the Index.

Your family may be mentioned or discussed in a source which is included in the *Newberry Library Genealogical Index*. Sources from specific states are listed after the general sources.

NEW ENGLAND HISTORICAL AND GENEALOGICAL REGISTER — VOL. 121 1967 | VOL. 120 1966 | VOL. 122 1968 | VOL. 123 1969 | VOL. 124 1970 | VOL. 125 1971 | VOL. 126 1972 | VOL. 127 1973

NORTH CAROLINA

Stanly observer. 1882–1891. w
No–Ar m s S 18,1884
NoGrE s S 18,1884
NcU s S 18,1884

APEX

Apex booster. [?] w
Nc–Ar m s N 25,1943–Jl 5,1945
NcGrE s N 25,1943–Jl 5,1945
NcU s N 25,1943–Jl 5,1945

ASHEBORO

Bulletin. 1905–1920? w
No–Ar m s 1914–1915
NoGrE s 1914–1915
NcU s 1914–1915

North Carolina bulletin. F 16,1856–1857? w
Nc–Ar m s F 16, Jl 12, Ag 9,1856; S 5,1857
NcGrE s F 16, Jl 12, Ag 9,1856; S 5,1857
NcU s F 16, Jl 12, Ag 9,1856; S 5,1857

Randolph herald. Ap 14,1846–1850? w
NcD m s [Ap 21,1846–Ap 12,1847]

Randolph regulator. F 2,1876–1879. w
Nc–Ar m s [F 2,1876–Mr 14,1877]; My 13,1879
NcGrE s [F 2,1876–Mr 14,1877]; My 13,1879
NcU s [F 2,1876–Mr 14,1877]; My 13,1879

Randolph sun. [?] w
Nc–Ar m s Jl 13,1878
NcGrE s Jl 13,1878
NcU s Jl 13,1878

Southern citizen. F 1846–1847? w
Continues Southern citizen and man of business.
No–Ar m s [F–N 1840; My–O 17,1844]
NcD s [F–N 1840; My–O 17,1844]
NcGrE s [F–N 1840; My–O 17,1844]
NcU s [F–N 1840; My–O 17,1844]
NcWsW s [F–N 1840; My–O 17,1844]

Southern citizen and man of business. D 31,1836–Ja 7 1840. w
Continued by Southern citizen.
Nc–Ar m s [1836–Ja 24,1840]
NcD s [1836–Ja 24,1840]
NcGrE s [1836–Ja 24,1840]
NcU s [1836–Ja 24,1840]
NcWsW s [1836–Ja 24,1840]

ASHEVILLE

Asheville advertiser. 1890. w
Nc–Ar m s S 20,1890
NcGrE s S 20,1890
NcU s S 20,1890

Asheville advocate. 1923?–1935. w
Continues Labor advocate.
Nc–Ar m s D 25,1931–O 11,1935
NcGrE s D 25,1931–O 11,1935

Asheville citizen-times. 1930– w
Joint Sunday edition of the Asheville citizen, and the Asheville daily times.
No microform reported

Asheville daily advance. 1883–1888. d
Nc–Ar m s Ag 13,1884; [F 22,1885–Ja 4,188?
NcGrE s Ag 13,1884; [F 22,1885–Ja 4,1888]
NcU s Ag 13,1884; [F 22,1885–Ja 4,1888]

Asheville daily gazette. 1892–1903. d
Continued by Asheville daily gazette-news.
No microform reported

Asheville daily gazette-news. 1903–F 19,1916.
Continues Asheville daily gazette.
Continued by Asheville daily times.
McP m 1904–1916

Asheville daily sun. Mr–Ag 7 1885. d
Title varies: Daily sun
Nc–Ar m s [My 31–Ag 5,1886]
NcGrE s [My 31–Ag 5,1886]
NcU s [My 31–Ag 5,1886]
NcWsW s [My 31–Ag 5,1886]

Asheville daily times. F 20,1916– d
Continues Asheville daily gazette-news.
Since 1930 the Sunday edition has been published jointly with the Asheville citizen, as Asheville citizen-times.
Title varies: Asheville times.
McP m 1916–
NcWsW s My 20,1923–O 20,1924

Asheville Democrat. O 10,1889–S 25,1892? w
Nc–Ar m s 1889–S 25,1892
NcGrE s 1889–S 25,1892
NcU s 1889–S 25,1892
NcWsW s 1889–S 25,1892

Asheville messenger. 1847?–1852? w
Continues Highland messenger.
NcA–S m [1847–Ag 27,1851]
NcU s [1847–Ag 27,1851]

Asheville news. 1849–1877? w
Continued by Asheville news and western farmer.
Nc–Ar m s [Ja 9,1851–1865]
NcGrE s [Ja 9,1851–1865]
NcU s [Ja 9,1851–1865]
NcWsW s [Ja 9,1851–1865]

Asheville news. 1860–1863. w
Nc–Ar m s O 20,1880; [Jl 18,1882–Mr 28,18
NcGrE s O 20,1880; [Jl 18,1882–Mr 28,1883
NcU s O 20,1880; [Jl 18,1882–Mr 28,1883]
NcWsW s O 20,1880; [Jl 18,1882–Mr 28,188

Asheville news and mountain farmer. 1869?–18
Continues Asheville news and western farm

Thorough research requires a search of the pertinent material related to the locale, the times, and the family in the genealogical periodicals. Here are a few volumes of America's oldest genealogical journal.

Information about the history of an ancestral locale and specific events may be discovered in community newspapers. The newspapers may be listed in *Newspapers in Microform*, which show specific library holdings.

OKEMAH

Okemah HERALD. sw Je 9 1933+
  OkHi [1933]+
  OkOk [1933]+

Okemah INDEPENDENT. *See* Okfuskee county
  news

Okemah LEADER. w Mr 1904-
  OkHi [1904-05]

Okemah daily LEADER. d 1925+
  pub [1926-27]+
  OkHi [1932]+
  OkOk [1928-29]+
  —w ed *See* Okemah ledger

Okemah LEDGER. w Ja 31 1907-32‖?
  Merged with Okfuskee county news
  OkHi [1907]-25
  —d ed *See* Okemah daily leader

OKFUSKEE county news. w S 9 1904+
  1904-14 as Okemah independent (title
  varies slightly)
  pub 1907+
  KHi Ja 26 1922
  OkHi [1904]-[14]+
  OkOk 1934+

SLEDGE hammer. w 1912-14‖?
  OkHi [1913-14]

OKLAHOMA CITY

Oklahoma City ADVERTISER. w 1931?+
  pub 1931+

AMERICAN guardian. w,d 1914+
  1914-Mr 27 1931 as Oklahoma leader (title
  varies slightly)
  d Ag 16 1920-Jl 23 1923
  pub 1931+
  CSt [1931-32]
  CSt-H [1930-32]
  CU-P F 17 1933+
  KHi Je 25 1926;Ag 19 1927
  MWA Jl 3 1931
  NNC F 1932-S 8 1933
  NNC-B F 1932+
  NNRa 1931-33
  NPV Jl 1931-F 10 1933
  OkHi [1918]-33
  OkOOk 1920+
  PP Ag 26 1932
  PUn [1932-33]
  WHi F 20 1925-Ag 18 1933

Daily BEACON of Capitol Hill. d Mr 5 1934?+
  pub 1934+
  OkHi 1934+

BLACK dispatch. w 1915+
  Negro
  pub 1915+
  OkHi [1916-17]+

BULL moose. w 1913‖?
  OkHi [1913]

CAPITAL American. w 1925-
  OkHi [1925-27]-31

Oklahoma City JOURNAL. d Je 3 1889-91‖?
  United with Daily times to form Oklahoma times-journal, later Oklahoma City
  times
  —w ed *See* Oklahoma journal

LIFE. *See* Oklahoma life

NEWS. *See* Oklahoma news

NEWS-STATE tribune. w -1911‖?
  OkHi 1910[11]

OKLAHOMA advance. w
  OkHi [1922]

OKLAHOMA champion. w Ja 1896-1900‖?
  United with Weekly Oklahoman to form
  Weekly Oklahoman and champion, later
  Weekly Oklahoman
  OkHi 1896-[1900]

OKLAHOMA chief. *See* State herald (Ardmore

OKLAHOMA citizen. w 1925?-
  OkHi [1926]-32

OKLAHOMA democrat. w 1890‖?
  OkHi [1890]

OKLAHOMA eagle. w
  OkHi [1906]

OKLAHOMA free daily pointer. *See* Oklahom
  City daily pointer

OKLAHOMA gazette. *See* Evening gazette

OKLAHOMA grit. *See* Grit

OKLAHOMA guide. w 1898-1903‖?
  Negro
  KHi O 1898-Jl 1 1903

OKLAHOMA journal. w My 9 1889-91‖?
  My 9 1889 as Oklahoma times (not to l
  confused with Oklahoma City times
  United with Oklahoma City times to for
  Oklahoma times-journal, later Week
  times-journal
  OkHi [1890-91]
  —d ed *See* Oklahoma City journal

OKLAHOMA leader. *See* American guardian

OKLAHOMA life. w 1902-09‖?
  1902-06? as Life
  1902-Ja 1906? pub in Anadarko
  OkHi [1903-08]

OKLAHOMA news. d O 1906+
  N 1-D 30 1916 as News
  pub 1906+
  KHi 1920-Ap 17 1929
  OkHi 1906[07-08;15]+
  OkOOk 1912+

OKLAHOMA pioneer. w 1883?-1915‖?
  In German
  OkHi [1893]-[95;1910-12]
  OkU My 11 1889

OKLAHOMA post. w 1901-07‖?
  Title varies: Oklahoma Saturday post
  OkHi [1901-02]-[07]

OKLAHOMA post. d 1906-07‖?
  OkHi [1906-07]

OKLAHOMA press. *See* Sunday press-recor

If microform editions of the community newspapers are not available, the copies may be in a courthouse or an archive. You may locate
these files or find clues to begin your search for them in Winifred
Gregory's 1934 publication, *American Newspapers*.

Special catalog files, which are locally prepared, are an aid for the historian and genealogist. An extensive file concerning a family or a locale may be found by consulting these card catalogs.

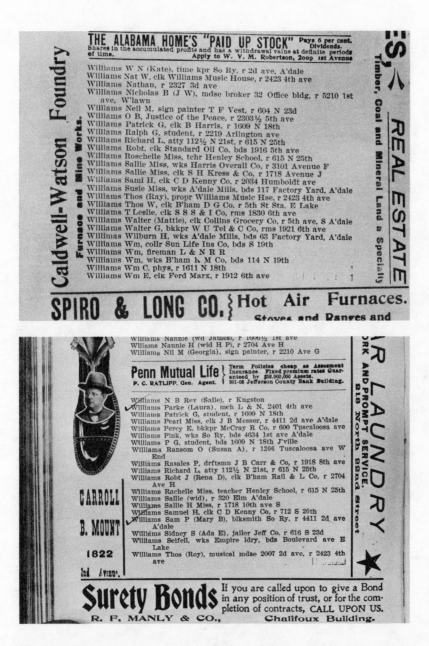

City directories may reflect the arrival and departure of persons in certain years; then research can be focused on a shorter time span in determining migration. Occupation, spouse, employer, and address are additional data in many directories.

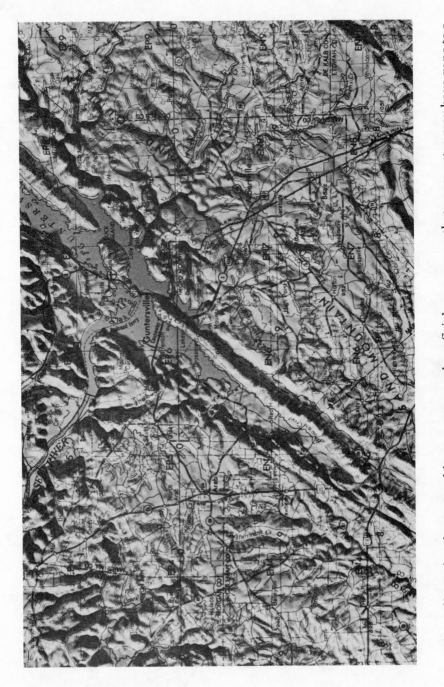

Three-dimensional topographic maps are very beneficial; you can see that an ancestor may have gone to a school, church, or community some distance from his home because of natural barriers.

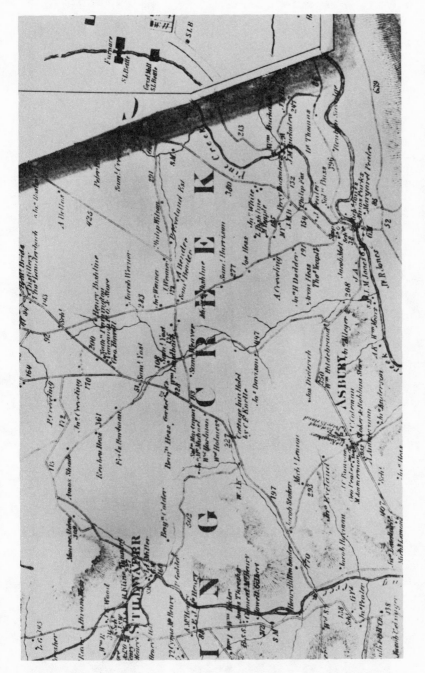

Real property maps of the 19th century and earlier are frequently of great value and interest to genealogical research. The location of my great-grandfather's homestead is designated on this portion of a Columbia County, Pennsylvania, map.

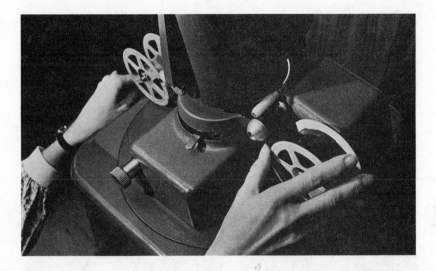

Threading the microfilm seems to be complex until it is done a few times. The step-by-step process is shown here. There are four basic points: (1) unwind the film from the bottom of the reel on this type of reader (some unwind from top), (2) pass between the two rollers, (3) draw between the two plastic discs, (4) pass between the two rollers on the opposite side and anchor the film on the take-up reel from the bottom again. (5) When the text is in position for reading, settle yourself comfortably to read the film and to take necessary notes.

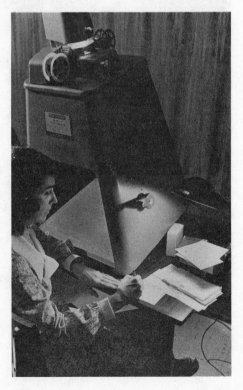

Selecting sources from the vast array of items in a research library is simplified when you choose categories of books and periodicals that should supply the necessary data. Here a helpful staff member indicates a South Carolina census index.

Card 1:

L 200 — ALABAMA

Leigh, John (HEAD OF FAMILY) VOL. 12 E.D. 169
SHEET 1 LINE 1
W M 49 Va.
(COLOR) (SEX) (AGE) (BIRTHPLACE)
Lawrence (COUNTY) Beat 7 Moulton (M.&D.)
(CITY) (STREET) (HOUSE NO.)

OTHER MEMBERS OF FAMILY

NAME	RELATIONSHIP	AGE	BIRTHPLACE
Leigh, H.C.	W	29	Ala
" G.G.	D	24	Ala
" E.A.	D	16	Tenn
" P.H.	S	9/12	Ala

1880 CENSUS—INDEX
DEPARTMENT OF COMMERCE
BUREAU OF THE CENSUS
A-1a

Card 2:

L 200 — STATE ALABAMA

Lacey, Jno (HEAD OF FAMILY) VOL. 19 E.D. 103
SHEET 51 LINE 32
B M 65 Virginia
(COLOR) (SEX) (AGE) (BIRTHPLACE)
Pickens (COUNTY) Beat 19 Franconia (M.&D.)
(CITY) (STREET) (HOUSE NO.)

OTHER MEMBERS OF FAMILY

NAME	RELATIONSHIP	AGE	BIRTHPLACE
Lacey, Sarah	W	67	South Carolina
Cureton, Limus	At S	10	Ala.

1880 CENSUS—INDEX
DEPARTMENT OF COMMERCE
BUREAU OF THE CENSUS
A-1a

Card 3:

L 200 — ALABAMA

Lewis, John (HEAD OF FAMILY) VOL. 17 E.D. 130
SHEET 18 LINE 20
W M 66 Va
(COLOR) (SEX) (AGE) (BIRTHPLACE)
Mobile
Foot of Mobile Adams
(CITY) (STREET) (HOUSE NO.)

OTHER MEMBERS OF FAMILY

NAME	RELATIONSHIP	AGE	BIRTHPLACE
Lewis Margaret	W	53	N.Y.
" Franklin	S	23	Ala

Soundex listings for the 1900 and 1880 censuses are helpful in locating information about your family. You must consult the census enumeration schedules for more complete information. Only families with children in the household below age 11 are included in the 1880 Soundex.

Computerized indexes are no substitute for a thorough examination of the census schedules, but they are of great assistance in pinpointing a person in the schedules. Be sure to extract the entries for all families of the surname in the same locale.

Page No. 2

SCHEDULE 3.—Persons who Died during the Year ending 1st June, 1860, in *South Madison District,* **in the County of** *Madison* **State of** *Alabama* **, enumerated by me,** *Hugh W. Coleman* **Ass't Marshal.**

		DESCRIPTION								
NAME OF EVERY PERSON WHO DIED during the year ending 1st June, 1860, whose usual place of abode at the time of death was in this family.	Age	Sex	Color (White, black, or mulatto)	Free or slave	Married or widowed	PLACE OF BIRTH, Naming the State, Territory, or Country.	THE MONTH in which the person died.	PROFESSION, OCCUPATION, OR TRADE.	DISEASE OR CAUSE OF DEATH.	NUMBER OF DAYS ILL.
1	2	3	4	5	6	7	8	9	10	11
1 Peggy Finnell	60	f	B	S		Unknown	Nov		Old age	
2 Sarah Finnell	1/2	f	B	S		Alabama	April		Spasms	1 day
3 Jerry Finnell	2	m	B	S		"	May		Cholera Morbus	1 day
4 Dempsy Finnell	22	m	B	S		"	"		Dropsy	6 mo
5 Byron "	3	m	B	S		"	"		Typhoid fever	1 mo
6 Jim "	3	m	B	S		"	June		"	3 mo
7 Willis "	65	m	B	S		Tennessee	"		Rheumatism	6 mo
8 Caldonia "	1	f	B	S		Alabama	Jan'y		Pneumonia	1 pm
9 James E. Turner	1	m				"	"		Sick Jaw	1 day
10 James R. Pleasants	1/2	m				"	April		Inflammation Bowels	1 mo
11 Peggy "	70	f	B	S		Mary Land	Jan		Old age	
12 John F Finnell	1/2	m				Alabama	March		Accident	instantly
13 Amelia McIntyre	59	f		W		Virginia	May		Dropsy of Chest	12 mo
14 Sallie Pride	4	f				Alabama	Dec		Hemorage	30 hrs
15 Aley Pride	19	f	B	S		"	Aug		Typhoid fever	5 w
16 Frances Clemens	3	f	B	S		"	Sept		Worms	4 mo
17 William Clemens	1	m	B	S		"	"		"	4 mo
18 Alice G Turner	5	f				"	Nov		Erysipelas	3 days
19 Elizabeth Sandifer	24	f			m	"	"		Typhoid fever	2 mo
20 Matty Patton	1	f	m	S		"	Feb		Bowel Disease	1 mo
21 Nash Patton	1/2	m	m	S		"	Oct		Dropsy	1 mo
22 Jordan Moore	18	m	m	S		"	July		Inflammation Bowels	2 mo
23 Madison Moore	21	m	m	S		"	Oct		Congestive Chill	1 day
24 Jefferson Moore	10	m	B	S		Virginia	June		Scrofula	3 mo
25 Indiana Moore	1/2	f	B	S		Alabama	Feb		Hives	1 mo
26 Richmond "	14	m	B	S		"	March		Scarlet fever	2 mo
27 Patty "	76	f	B	S		Virginia	May		Old age	
28 Robertson Bruce	41	m		W		Georgia	July	Queen	Inflammation Bowels	1 mo
29 Martha E. Smith	15	f				Alabama	Nov		Bowel Disease	2 mo
30 Mary A. Smith	45	f		m		Georgia	Jan'y		Typhoid fever	2 mo
31 Almond Atkinson	60	m		m		Virginia	"	Farmer	Congestive Chill	1 day
32										
33										
34										
35										

Total number of deaths — No. of white males / No. of white females — No. of black males 11 / No. of black females 7 — No. of mulatto males / No. of mulatto females — Total male slaves / Total female slaves — No. of married / No. of widowed

REMARKS:

Details regarding age, place of birth, month of death, occupation, and cause of death are included in the Mortality Schedules for the decennial years. These were taken separately in conjunction with the censuses of 1850 to 1880 and the limited census of 1885.

HVS-20109—75M—9-57 ⬤—10
(Fee for this
Certificate, $1.00)

This is to Certify that the following is a true and correct copy of a certificate of death
filed in the Vital Statistics Section, Pennsylvania Department of Health, as directed
by Act 66 of the General Assembly, 1953, P. L. 304.

Nº 540405

JUL 1 4 1969
(Date)

Thomas W Georgesh MD
(Secretary of Health)

COMMONWEALTH OF PENNSYLVANIA
DEPARTMENT OF HEALTH
VITAL STATISTICS

File No. *117052-30*

Primary
Dist No. *40-08-41*

CERTIFICATE OF DEATH

Registered No. *2*

1. PLACE OF DEATH a. County *Luzerne*	2. USUAL RESIDENCE (where deceased lived. If institution: residence before admission) a. State *Pa.* b. County *Luzerne*
c. City, Borough or Township *Forty-Fort*	c. Length of stay in 1b.	c. City, Borough or Township *Forty Fort*
d. FULL NAME (If not in hospital, give street address) of HOSPITAL or INSTITUTION *105 Fort St.*	d. Street Address or Location *105 Fort St*
e. Is Place of Death Inside Municipality Limits? Yes ☐ No ☐	e. Is Residence Inside Municipality Limits? Yes ☐ No ☐ f. Is Residence on a Farm? Yes ☐ No ☐

3. NAME OF DECEASED (Type or print) a. (First) *Edward* b. (Middle) *M* c. (Last) *Brobst*	4. DATE OF DEATH (Month) (Day) (Year) *Dec. 24 1930*
5. SEX *male*	6. COLOR OR RACE *white*	7. MARRIED ☐ NEVER MARRIED ☐ WIDOWED ☒ DIVORCED ☐	8. DATE OF BIRTH *11-21-1853*	9. AGE (in years last birthday) *77*	If under 1 year Months Days	If under 24 hrs. Hours Min.

10. FULL NAME OF SPOUSE	11. BIRTHPLACE (Also give state or foreign country) *Black Haven Pa.*	12. CITIZEN OF WHAT COUNTRY

13. FATHER'S NAME *George Brobst* Born *Pa.*	14. MOTHER'S MAIDEN NAME — *Billheimer* Born *Pa.*
15. USUAL OCCUPATION (even if retired) *Laborer*	16. Social Security No.	17. INFORMANT *Grant Stackhouse* ADDRESS *6 3rd Pittston Pa.*

MEDICAL CERTIFICATION

Interval Between
Onset and Death

18. CAUSE OF DEATH [Enter only one cause per line for (a), (b) & (c)] PART 1. Death was caused by:	
IMMEDIATE CAUSE (a) *Acute Bilateral Broncho Pneumonia*	*2 days*
Conditions, if any, which gave rise to above cause (a) stating the underlying cause last. DUE TO (b)	
DUE TO (c) *Acute Bronchitis*	

PART 11. OTHER SIGNIFICANT CONDITIONS [contributing to death but not related to the terminal disease given in Part 1 (a)]

19. WAS AUTOPSY PERFORMED?
Yes ☐ No ☒

20a. ACCIDENT SUICIDE HOMI-CIDE ☐ ☐ ☐	20b. DESCRIBE HOW INJURY OCCURRED	20c. Time of Injury Hour, m. E.S.T.	Month, Day, Year
20d. INJURY OCCURRED While at work ☐ Not while at work ☐	20e. PLACE OF INJURY (e.g., home, farm, factory, street, etc.)	20f. CITY, BOROUGH, TOWNSHIP COUNTY STATE

21. I hereby certify that I attended the deceased from *12/23/*, 19*30*, to *12/24/*19*30* that I last saw the deceased alive on *12/24/*19*30*, and that death occurred at *4 P.* m., E.S.T., from the causes and on the date stated above.

22a. SIGNATURE *Edward I Wolfe* M.D. or D.O. 22b. ADDRESS *Forty Fort Pa.*	22c. DATE SIGNED *12/27/30*
23a. BURIAL ☒ CREMATION ☐ REMOVAL ☐	23b. DATE *12/27/30*	23c. NAME OF CEMETERY OR CREMATORY *Hanover Cem*	23d. LOCATION (City, Boro., Twp. & County) (State)
24. DATE REC'D BY REG. *12/27/30*	25. REGISTRAR'S SIGNATURE *H. H. Hadsall*	26. SIGNATURE OF FUNERAL DIRECTOR *Wm. Grindrod.* ADDRESS *W. Pittston Pa.*

If available, death certificates should be obtained for all family members as they reveal a great deal of information. Additional data that may be beneficial include the birthdate, birthplace, age, citizenship, mother's maiden name, and name and address of informant.

HANOVER CEMETERY, WILKES-BARRE, PA

Edward Brobst - Lot. 345 S.1/2 - 6 graves - July 19 (1907) *$35.00

	Age	Date of Death	Date of Inter.	Place of Birth	Last Residence
N.1 George A. Brobst	56	7-28-51	7-31-51	Kingston	Pittston
N.2 Alice A. Stackhouse	43	4-20-33	4-22-33		West Pittston
N.3 Grant Stackhouse	64	9-7-55	9-10-55	Unityville	West Pittston
S.1 Pearl Brobst	71	9-10-55	9-12-55	?	Bloomsburg
S.2 Edward Brobst	77	12-24-30	12-27-30		Forty Fort
S.3 Anna Brobst	45	1901	(1901)		

C.E. Brobst — Lot. S.W.1/2 115 — 6 graves — June 29-1894 — *$5.00

	Age	Date of Death	Date of Inter.	Place of Birth	Last Residence
S.1 Lena M. Brobst	Baby	1894			
S.2 Russell W. Brobst	9	1901			
S.5 Mary K. Brobst	79	3-3-44	3-6-44		Kingston
S.6 Clarence F. Brobst	69	2-28-29	3-1-29		Kingston

A sexton's records can be more useful than tombstone inscriptions, as they may provide information about the birthplace and the last residence of the deceased. Sometimes they reveal data on related families that is unknown to the researcher.

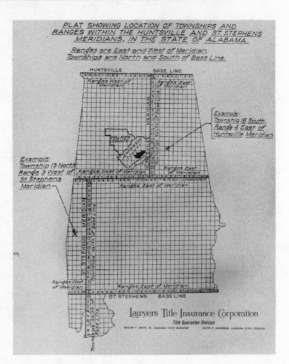

Title and abstract companies have a supply of public-land survey maps pertaining to their geographic interests. This one shows the two principal meridians upon which the descriptions of public lands are based in Alabama.

110

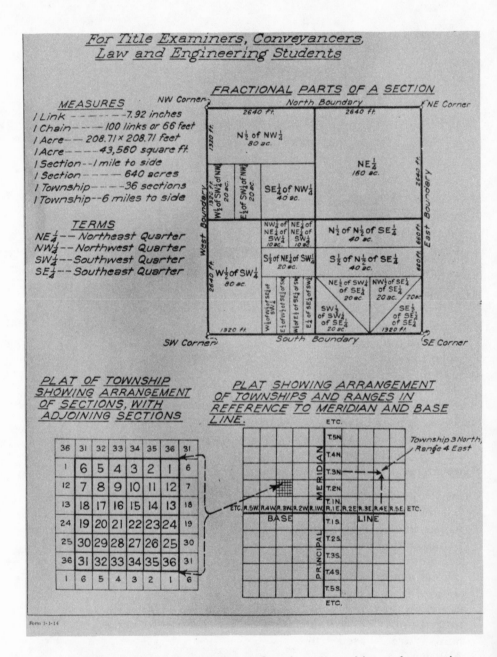

This shows the arrangement of sections, townships and ranges in relation to the meridian and base lines, and the terms that are used to describe fractional parts of a section.

The record room of this courthouse shows a typical series of bound files of marriages, probate records, and accompanying indexes. Volumes are usually large and heavy. Here, a staff member shows how to check an index for data about a family member.

Genealogists often find important information in the case files, which are usually stacked row upon row in the record rooms or storage areas of county courthouses. This photograph shows a document being examined by a helpful staff member.

Probate case files may yield valuable family data. The administratrix has set forth in this document the entire living family of the deceased; ages and city of residence of each family member are listed.

Various reports and actions concerning guardianship activities are recorded in minutes of the court. Three successive guardians are named in this short portion of the record.

Tract books record the original grants of land in public-land states as they were reported by the Register of Public Lands to the Secretary of State in each respective state. Listings are by section in order of the townships; they give the original grantee's name, date of sale, and certificate or warrant number. The state title is identified by name of person and the date it was conveyed.

This direct index to records of deeds, mortgages, and other instruments is alphabetized by the first letter only of the grantor's surname, reflecting the type of record filed, date of filing, and the volume and page where the instrument is recorded.

A typical land description of a public-land state appears in this indenture in which John Harper and James Webb sold to Edmond F. Lyon a parcel in Tuscaloosa County, AL, on 29 December 1826. It consisted of the "west half of the southwest quarter of section ten in township twenty three of range five east"; this may be abbreviated W 1/2 SW 1/4 S 10 T 23 R 5 E.

I, Basil Manly of Charleston, in the State of South
Carolina, do make and ordain this my last Will, and Testament, hereby revoking, and making void all former Wills,
by me at any time made: viz.

First, After the payment of my just debts, I give and
bequeath all the residue of the property of which I may be
possessed, both real and personal, or to which I may here-
after have or acquire any title, to my Wife, Sarah
Murray Manly, absolutely, and in fee simple; confi-
ding in the wisdom, justice and goodness of my said
Wife to make such distribution to our children, as their
wants may require, and as the condition of the estate
may allow. —

Second, I appoint my aforesaid wife, Sarah Murray
Manly, sole Executrix of this my last Will and Testament.

In Testimony whereof, I have hereunto set my
hand and seal this twenty third day of July, in the
year of our Lord One thousand, eight hundred and
fifty eight.

        B. Manly {Seal}

Signed, sealed, published and declared by the said
Basil Manly as and for his last will and testament, in
the presence of us, who at his request and in his presence,
& in the presence of each other, have subscribed our names
as witnesses hereunto.

        William B. Heriot

        B. I. Whaley

        William Thayer

Some wills are straightforward, uncomplicated, and may yield
little ancestral information. The will of Basil Manly simply leaves his
entire estate to his wife, Sarah Murray. It is witnessed by William B.
Heriot, B. I. Whaley, and William Thayer (or perhaps Hayes).

Estate inventories reflect the occupation and lifestyle of a deceased person. The names of slaves are particularly important to correlate with other family records.

An interesting document records the marriage of Samuel Abernathy to Eleanor Abernathy on 20 August 1825 in accordance with a license obtained on 16 August 1825. The marriage was solemnized by Hosea Holcombe, a pioneer Baptist minister.

Some church records may contain valuable information about family members; other records may be disappointing in their lack of information. A simple search for names may not yield very much, but a careful examination may reward the researcher.

This pension application contains rather extensive data about the applicant, Rowland Estes, who declares that he served nearly three years in the American Revolution in Captain Richard Stephens' Company, 10th Regiment of the Virginia line.

Left card:

P. | 11 | Ind.

Jacob Pollem

Appears with rank of *Private* on

Muster and Descriptive Roll of a Detachment of U. S. Vols. forwarded

for the *11* Reg't Indiana Infantry. Roll dated *Indianapolis, Ind Mar 2* 186*5*.

Where born *Richland Co. Ohio*.

Age *27* years; occupation *Farmer*

When enlisted *Feb. 9*, 186*5*.

Where enlisted *Indianapolis*

For what period enlisted *one* years.

Eyes *blue*; hair *light*

Complexion *fair*, height *5* ft. *9* in.

When mustered in *Feb. 14*, 186*5*.

Where mustered in *Indianapolis*

Bounty paid $ *33 1/3* 100; due $ *66 2/3* 100

Where credited *Columbia Tp.*

Whitley Co. 10 Cong. Dist.

Company to which assigned *H*

Remarks:

Book mark:

Ripps Copyist.

(339)

Right card:

P | 11 | Ind.

Jacob R Pollom

Pvt., Co. *H*, 11 Reg't Indiana Infantry.

Age *27* years.

Appears on **Co. Muster-out Roll,** dated *Baltimore Md July 26*, 186*5*.

Muster-out to date *July 26*, 186*5*.

Last paid to *Apl 30*, 186*5*.

Clothing account:

Last settled , 186 ; drawn since $ 100

Due soldier $ 100; due U. S. $ *4 65* 100

Am't for cloth'g in kind or money adv'd $ 100

Due U. S. for arms, equipments, &c., $ 100

Bounty paid $ *33 1/3* 100; due $ 100

Remarks:

Book mark:

Black Copyist.

(361)

This is part of the Civil War military record of Jacob R. Pollem, Private, Company H, 11th Regiment, Indiana Infantry. Notice that Private Pollem's name is incorrectly spelled on the muster-out roll. There is only a brief description of the person, but details about mustering and the location of the home county are given.

Occupation, age, and country of origin are frequently indicated on passenger lists. The ship *North America* sailed from Liverpool, England, and arrived in the port of New York 28 September 1842. The Fagan and Parker families are among those listed.

| 1851–'52. | | 410 |

[No. 281.] AN ACT

For the relief of the heirs of James English, deceased.

SEC. 1. *Be it enacted by the Senate and House of Representatives of the State of Alabama in General Assembly convened,* That Thomas English, Sarah Densmore, formerly Sarah English, Hannah English, Mary English, and the other brothers and sisters, if any, and the descendants of such as may be deceased, of James English, deceased, be and they are hereby deemed capable of inheriting any property of which the said James English died possessed in this state as fully and effectually as if they were citizens of the United States.

Capable of inheriting.

SEC. 2. *And be it further enacted,* That the property, real and personal, of the estate of the said James English shall be distributed among his heirs in the same manner and under the same rules and regulations as the estates of other deceased persons are by the laws of this state: *Provided,* Nothing in this act shall be so construed as to affect the rights of creditors.

Distribution of property.

APPROVED, January 28, 1852.

Legislative acts concerning estates were common in pre-Civil War days; they provided relief for families or widows in connection with the inheritance laws. These actions are now usually handled by probate or other courts.

Military Records

Your ancestors may have played some roles in the wars of history. Great quantities of records are usually generated during wars. You may use records of registration for military draft, enlistment, promotion, transfer, discharge, military units, and other wartime activities in your family research. The data in these records will give you important information for your family biographies.

You should begin with the most current records. Some records may be restricted for 75 years from the date of a person's separation from the service, and thus not open for your examination. However, you may get information from these military records by requesting it from the National Personnel Records Center, 9700 Page Blvd., St. Louis, MO 63132. You may request Navy officers' records if they were discharged after 1902, by writing to the Bureau of Naval Personnel, Department of the Navy, Washington, DC 20350. You should remember that the Navy and the Marine Corps are separate from the Army. Since World War II, the Air Force has also had separate status.

Draft Records

If you know your relative's residence, at least within the area of a specific Selective Service Board of World War I, you can get copies of an individual's draft registration from the Federal Archives and Records Center, GSA, East Point, GA 30344. The draft record gives the full name, street address, age, birthdate, race, citizenship, occupation, employer and address, nearest relative and address, and signature.

If your relative was ultimately subject to the draft, you will find more detailed information in a questionnaire completed for the board. Conscription for military service in World War I began on 5 June 1917 when men ages 21 to 30 were registered. Later, men between the ages of 17 and 45 were registered, but the actual draft did not include the extremes of age classes.

Review your family group sheets now, and list members who might have been subject to the draft in each American war. List the name of your relative, his age at the war's onset, and any known military or civilian service.

If you determine, for example, that your relative was eligible for conscription in either Union or Confederate service, you should search for Civil War draft records. Conscription for military service in the Civil War started with the Confederate States. Some states enacted enrollment laws for the state militia before the war began in April 1861. North Carolina drafted men aged 18 to 45 to the state militia. When the Confederate Government was formed, the state militia may have been transferred to the Confederate command with changes in officer and enlisted personnel.

The Confederacy began conscription of men aged 18 to 35 by a law dated 16 April 1862, which was amended on 11 October 1862, providing extensive exemption. The age limit was extended to 45, and in later acts it was further expanded from 17 to 50. The Federal Government Enrollment Act of 3 March 1863 required registration of men aged 20 to 45; it was later broadened.

The National Archives has the Federal draft records of the Civil War. Consolidated enrollment lists prepared in the states were sent to headquarters in Washington, D.C. They are arranged by state and divided by Congressional (enrollment) district; they are also alphabetically arranged by the initial letter of the surname. These records show name, residence, age as of 1 July 1863, occupation, marital status, and the state, territory, or country of birth. They may also identify a military unit that he previously served in, or the one in which he subsequently served. Descriptive rolls of drafted men are available for each district; some are indexed. These records frequently show a description of the man, his exact place of birth, and his acceptance or rejection for service. Many volumes contain incomplete entries. Determine the district in which he resided from the *Congressional Directory* published in 1865. You must know his place of residence at the time of registration.

The Confederate draft records are not usually preserved; however, they may be in the respective state archives for some states.

The War of 1812, fought by a young nation barely consolidated from its disparate colonial roots and customs, ultimately brought about congressional debates on conscription. However, no federal draft law was enacted, but some states enacted a form of draft.

The Revolutionary War was fought with a combination of Continental forces and units of colonial militias. Massachusetts and Virginia each conscripted for the war in 1777. Their example caused Congress to commend their conscriptions to the other colonies. Colonial conscription records, if extant, may be in the respective state archives.

Military Records—World War I Back to the Civil War

Major military actions between the Civil War and World War I may have involved an ancestor of yours. An ancestor may have served in one of the following wars: the Philippine

Insurrection (1899–1902), the Spanish-American War (1898–99), or Indian Wars after the Civil War. Check to see whether a family member served in one of these wars. There were relatively few men involved in these operations. These records are in the National Archives. The National Archives will provide you with printed booklets and forms to assist your research. Visit or write the archives for this phase of your research.

Civil War Records of Union Personnel

Since the Civil War was an internecine strife, the records of the Union and Confederate personnel are in separate collections and differ in arrangement, content, and inclusiveness. Your family may need to use only one of these collections, but, in many families, brother fought against brother or cousin against cousin.

Two major collections of records deal with Union personnel. Service records offer data of individuals serving in the military. Veterans' records offer data not only regarding military service, but of family members, comrades, and acquaintances involved in the pension process. Consult these records in person, or submit GSA Form 6751 to the National Archives, Washington, D.C. 20408. Before you visit or write, you should review the data for each family member who is listed in the "Veterans' Schedules" of the 1890 census. The schedules identify the military unit of each individual veteran or the widow surviving at that time. (Unfortunately, the schedules for the states [alphabetically] of Alabama through half of Kentucky were lost or destroyed).

You can then use the "Organizational Pension Index," which is easier to search than the alphabetical name index. However, you should verify the file numbers with the alphabetical index. A "Remarried Widows Index" (second part), available only to National Archives personnel, may also be beneficial in some cases.

Southern Records in the National Archives

While county histories of the period from 1875 to about 1900 supply much biographical information for many counties of the northern and midwestern states, relatively few histories were published for the southern states. Thus, the Confederate records in the National Archives, and the State Archives of former Confederate States (which are admittedly incomplete), are auxiliary sources if you have southern ancestry.

You should also check the "Confederate Citizens File," which relates to the correspondence of individuals with the Confederate War Department. Included in this file are bills and vouchers for services and supplies furnished to the Confederate government, and papers for damage claims against it. This file is sometimes cross referenced to other Confederate records. The files are arranged alphabetically by name of person or firm. You will find them on microfilm in some major libraries. You might obtain helpful data, including names, residences, dates, and other information from these files.

As each specific area came under federal control, the Union provost marshals developed records with data on residents of the area. You will find in the "Union Provost Marshal Civilians File" correspondence, reports, lists, affidavits, loyalty oaths, claims for property used or taken by Union military authorities or for supplies or services furnished the army, papers relating to civilian and some military prisoners, travel authorizations within the Confederate States, and postwar papers. The alphabetically arranged microfilms are available in some libraries. You may find data such as name, residence, date, and other details appropriate to the type of document.

You should also check the "Amnesty Oaths." You may find the following data: name, place of taking oath (often the residence), date of oath, and the signature of the person taking the oath. Some records include the person's age, personal description, and sometimes the identity of his Confederate military unit. The information about his residence may enable you to locate the family in the 1860 and 1870 censuses.

Another set of records, "Amnesty Papers," contains applications for presidential pardons for former Confederate officials or for persons owning property valued at twenty thousand dollars or more. These individuals were considered leaders in the Confederacy. Supporting documents were required with these amnesty applications. You may find extensive data for your family history in examining the appropriate papers. Alphabetical lists by states were published in the Congressional Serial Set, which is available in many depository libraries. These libraries are designated officially as sources for and repositories of government publications.

Cotton bills of sale, vouchers, and registers and lists of cotton sales for the years 1862–65 reveal transactions between individual cotton sellers and the Confederate government. A name index was published in Congressional number 6348; it may be consulted in a government depository library or on microfilm at some libraries. Each entry shows the name, county or parish, number of bales sold, value in Confederate currency or bonds, and date.

Military Records of Confederates

You may find useful information in the National Archives' collection of records related to Confederate military service and other records.

The "Compiled Military Service Records" consist of card abstracts from muster pay and some original papers which may include the name, state, company and regiment, rank, date and place of enlistment and discharge, occupation, personal description, along with details of capture, release, parole, or death. The indexes and records have been microfilmed, and are in some southern libraries and most southern state archives.

"Records Relating to Naval and Marine Personnel" consist of cards and papers relating to individuals in naval or marine service for the Confederacy. The records show the name, ship or station, date and place of capture, cause of admission to a hospital, and date of discharge. Some of these records have been microfilmed.

"Reference Cards and Papers" are records related to either naval or marine personnel. These records, now microfilmed, show the name, rank, and references to other records. Although the records are incomplete, you may use them chiefly as a guide to other records.

"Shipping Articles," a single volume with typed index, consists of shipping articles (agreements between the shipmaster and the crewmen that are similar to enlistment papers) of some enlisted men in the Confederate Navy. They show the name, rating, signature, and enlistment date. Thus, you get confirmation of a name, an evaluation of your ancestor's seamanship or related ability, a signature, and the location of an individual on that particular date.

Pension Records and State Records of Confederate Veterans

Individual states of the Confederacy have gathered records in their respective state archives that are related to veterans of the Civil War. These sometimes supplement or substitute for records that may be found in the National Archives. Confederate military archival material may be in repositories such as the Confederate Memorial Building (United Daughters of the Confederacy—U.D.C.) in Richmond, Virginia, in library manuscript collections, or in private collections.

You should begin with the pension records and work back to the service records in your search for military records.

Remember that officers' records are usually more extensive than those of enlisted personnel, and all of the records of an officer should be obtained. Your relative's service in one military unit may be separate from his service in another unit. Furthermore, courts-martial and some medical records are separate from all other records and require a separate search.

You should usually check these sources in the following order: the state archives, the National Archives, the Confederate Memorial Building, the library manuscript collections of the state and region, and finally private collections.

Pensions were paid by the states until 1958, and not by the Federal Government. State pension records provide helpful information on the individual, and on anyone whose statements or papers are contained in his pension file.

State censuses of living Confederate veterans are important to link with the pension and service records. For example, Alabama took a census of the veterans in 1907. These special censuses are gradually being published in genealogical periodicals.

Since 26 February 1929, Congress has received applications for headstones for Confederate veterans, previously excluded from consideration. These application records are in case files and arranged alphabetically. They record the name, organization, date of death, place of burial, and the name and address of the person requesting the headstone. Obviously, they may be helpful since about a half century has passed, and family records may not give these facts.

Military Records Since the American Revolution

Major military actions taking place between the Revolution and the Civil War may have involved members of your family if they were in this country. Did your ancestor serve in

the various Indian Wars before the Civil War, the Mexican
War (1846–48), or the War of 1812 (1812–15)?

Check his service record in these wars. Records in the
National Archives may supply useful information. Often,
there are indexes, printed rosters, and other aids to assist
you in locating the records. Three major collections of
records apply to these wars: (1) Service records of the war;
(2) Veterans' records in four series: a. The "Old Wars" Series
of Death and Disability Files; b. The War of 1812 Series; c.
The Mexican War Series; d. The Indian Wars Series. Some
of these files may be found through the "Remarried Widows
Index" (first part). (3) Bounty-land warrant application files
based on wartime service from 1775 to 3 March 1855. Some
claims have been interfiled with the veteran's pension
claims.

The Revolutionary War

If a relative served in the Revolutionary War, records may
be in two separate repositories. If he served in the Continental Army, Navy, or Marine units of the provisional government, his record may be in the National Archives. If he
served in the state troops rather than in the Continental
service, his record may be in the state archives, at the National Archives, or both. However, many records have been
destroyed by fire. The compiled records are based on substantial but incomplete collections of papers and records
related to the Revolutionary War, which were gathered over
the years after the fires.

Two kinds of veterans' benefits were granted: (1) pensions
and (2) bounty land. The pensions were granted in expand-
ing categories to invalid or disabled veterans, widows and
orphans of men who died in service, aged veterans, and
aged widows. Thus, you will find death or disability pen-

sions and service pensions in these compiled records. These pensions resulted from a series of congressional acts from 1789 through the mid-1800s. Although the Federal Government assumed many early pensions that had been granted by certain states, most of the early federal records were destroyed by fires in Washington, D.C., in November 1800 and August 1814. Few Revolutionary pension applications in existence date before 1800.

Free land was promised as an inducement to men to serve or to continue to serve in the Revolutionary War, because there was insufficient money to pay them. The Continental Congress began this practice with a resolution dated 16 September 1776, which promised free land to those who would serve in the war and to dependents (widows or children) of those who were killed by the enemy. The provisions eventually stipulated that 100 acres would be granted to each enlisted man, and 200 to each lieutenant, and increased by rank to 1,100 acres to a major general. Land warrants (rights to land) were authorized 9 July 1788, and time extensions for perfecting claims were granted in later years. On 3 March 1855, Congress approved the extension of bounty-land warrant benefits, increased the acreage allowance to 160 acres (a quarter-section), and reduced the minimum service period to 14 days or service in any battle. Naval service was similarly rewarded on 14 May 1856. Many applications resulted from this expanded eligibility and increased acreage; these claims were filed mainly by descendants of the veterans.

Prior to these mid-century acts, most warrants were converted for tracts of land in two specific areas: The United States Military District of Ohio, or for Virginia warrants (federally recognized) in the Virginia Military District of Ohio. Warrant owners were authorized later to exchange these earlier warrants for scrip and to obtain land in other areas of the public domain.

The *Index of Revolutionary War Pension Applications,* published by the National Genealogical Society (1976 edition), facilitates the use of these records when you want to obtain copies of pages from pension or bounty-land warrant applications. The entire collection is available on microfilm in some major libraries.

Regular Military Service

Your family may have had some members who served in the regular military service. Information about these persons may be in the records of the regular establishment at the National Archives. Records of their service are in numerous series of War Department records, but these records basically consist of enlisted records and officer records. Enlisted men's records include enlistment papers (1818 to 31 October 1912), and enlistment registers (1793–1914). After 1894, the records contain more complete information. Officer records include unindexed correspondence files (1800–1863), some consolidated files (1863–1889), and some separate files (1890 to 15 June 1912). Officer files may contain letters in which the marital status, family size, or residence is identified.

All of these records may be of value. If they record successive changes of post, you may obtain clues to locations of marriage records, births of children, deaths, and burials.

Colonial Wars

The colonial wars gained and protected the freedom of the colonists from the encroachment of France, Spain, and the Indians. This effort prepared the way for the War of Independence from Great Britain.

Unless your ancestors immigrated later than the Revolution, you may already know about family members who were involved in the colonial wars. Perhaps you may be unaware of family participation in the Pennamite War, Pontiac's War, the French and Indian War and others. Should your family lines in America antedate the Revolutionary War, you should check to determine if a family member participated in one of the colonial wars.

Once you have determined your ancestor's residence (the colony), you can undertake a search of the colony's records. These are housed in the archives of the state, which succeeded the colonial government of the area. Many of the public documents of this period have been published in archives or record series by the state. These published archives are in many major libraries throughout the nation; you may uncover interesting resources for this phase of your research by visiting a library. Also, substantial collections of papers in England relating to the colonies might yield data for your search. Much of this material is now microfilmed, and copies are in some major libraries. As you work back to this colonial period in your family search, you undoubtedly will gain rich historical information as well as genealogical data.

Keeping the Peace

Once a war is over, the interim military government and the new civilian government each create substantial records; these should not be overlooked. This transition may generate an abundance of records which may prove useful in your genealogical research.

Two significant activities during a war are likely to be disregarded by the family historian. They are the civilian aspects of the government such as record keeping, education, and morale and war-related activities such as production and manpower. Learn to ferret out the records, understand them, and apply them to your family research.

Most wars are not unanimously supported by the people. There are even unpopular wars such as the one in Viet Nam. Religious groups such as Quakers and Mennonites frequently become involved in conscientious objectors' movements. But you must not *assume* that a Quaker ancestor did not take up arms; many did. During a war, records are usually maintained on conscientious objectors. These records must be examined if you have an ancestor who was a pacifist or conscientious objector. After amnesty has been granted, detailed records will be very helpful to your research.

Through the use of military records, we have been able to assemble a great deal of family information. Service records of many relatives have been obtained. Finding identical names in the records creates confusion during our search. This leads to closer examination of information about our family members. Correlation of information from other records, such as pension applications, censuses, county histories, marriage records, regimental histories, and church records, is necessary to a full appreciation of the whole range of family information.

Public Land Records

Your search of the deeds in the courthouse may lead you to the federal land records. When the United States of America was formed, individual colonies ceded certain land to the Federal Government. Some of the colonies retained certain territory out of which other states were formed— Tennessee from North Carolina; Kentucky and West Virginia from Virginia; Maine from Massachusetts; and Vermont from land disputed between New Hampshire and New York. All of these were private-land or state-land states.

The rest of the country became public domain subject to disposal by the Federal Government. The public-land states were created from this public domain over the course of more than a century. These states include all of those west of the Mississippi River (except Texas), all states north of the Ohio River, and the states of Florida, Alabama, Mississippi, and Alaska. Texas should be considered a state-land state. Texas was brought into the United States with an agreement that the state could retain its land; records are at the General Land Office in Austin.

You may be surprised to learn that the great majority of adult males in the country before 1835 or thereabouts had abundant opportunity to obtain land. Thus, their names may appear somewhere in the land records. In private-land or state-land states, records are in the county or state files and not in the federal files.

Records of the public-land states are in the Bureau of Land Management (formerly General Land Office) Archives in Silver Spring, Maryland, or at the Washington National Records Center in Suitland, Maryland. There are many links between the records at the National Archives and those at the public land record depositories. Transportation between these facilities is provided by the National Archives.

The federal records that relate to public lands include separate files for credit entry, cash entry, donation entry, military bounty land, homestead entry, and private land claims. The donation entries are similar to homestead entries. The private land claims are based on grants or settlements before the nation officially held the territory. Spanish, French, and British grants were the basis for private land claims in Alabama and Mississippi, and French grants were the basis for claims in the Northwest Territory (now Illinois, Indiana, Michigan, and Wisconsin). The military bounty-land records are distinct from the bounty-land warrant application files described earlier.

You must determine the appropriate files to examine for your family search. Understanding the land-grant process is essential to thorough use of these records. Local land office records include cash books, journals, receiver's ledgers, registers of certificates, sale records, land warrant location records, tract books, and letter files. To use these may require professional knowledge. It's best that you undertake research in the public land records in the Washington area, *after* searching the county deed records.

To prepare for your research visit, carefully read a detailed introduction to these records. When you enter the National Archives, seek the aid of experienced research advisers. You will find final certificates to be most helpful. A final certificate normally shows the name and place of residence at time of purchase, the acreage of tract purchased, the description by subdivision, section, township, and range, summary of payments, and a citation to the volume and page of the patent record. Land patents issued to the owner were the final step in the process. Many families who acquired public land have passed the patents on to descendants.

If your ancestor had a preemption (prior right) claim, he had to provide proof of this fact. This proof record includes the number and relationship of household members, and a description of improvements made to the property.

If your ancestor obtained land in Florida (1842–1850) or Oregon or Washington (Dec. 1850–Nov. 1853), the file should contain a permit to settle, an application for a patent, a report by the land agent, and a final certificate. The permit to settle shows his name, marital status, month and year he became a resident, and land description. The land patent application shows his name, land description, settler's name (often different from the applicant), and period of his settlement. The final certificate shows information previously described, and a reference to the volume and page of the patent record.

The Oregon-Washington donation land entry files show three other items of special value: date and place of birth, the given name of a wife, and the date and place of marriage.

If you are searching in the Midwest or the far west, you may need to focus on the homestead entry files. Much of the land was obtained by homesteading under the act of 20 May 1862, or in later acts. Modifications were made by subsequent acts, such as one enacted on 8 June 1872 that authorized special benefits for Union veterans or their widows and orphans. Your ancestor's homestead application should show his name, residence, and the description and size of tract. His homestead proof record includes a tract description, his name, age, post office address, and house description; it also shows the date his residence was established, number and relationship of family members, crop description, and acreage under cultivation. His final certificate shows tract location, his name, post office address, the date the patent was issued, and a citation to the patent record. If he was a naturalized citizen, the proceedings of his naturalization or his declared intention to become a citizen show the name, date and port of arrival, and place of birth. If he obtained ownership by cash purchase before the minimum time required by homestead law, the papers will be filed with the cash entry files of the same land office.

If you have an ancestor who served in the Revolutionary War, the War of 1812, or in a war prior to 3 March 1855, he may have obtained a bounty-land warrant. Warrants were issued to certain veterans of service, their heirs, or assignees between 1775 and 1855. Applications for warrants required specified information, and they had to be approved. Virginia issued warrants to certain Revolutionary War veterans, their heirs, or assignees. Similarly, these had to be approved by the Virginia government, and were later recognized by the Federal Government.

Until 1842, the War of 1812 warrants could not be assigned. Many of the veterans or their heirs sold the warrants on the open market, and did not settle on the public domain. You may be fortunate if your ancestor used his warrant to settle on specified public land. After 1830, Revolutionary War warrants could be exchanged for scrip certificates. These certificates could be used to acquire land elsewhere in the public domain, in place of a specific area reserved for the veterans such as the Military District of Ohio. From 1842 warrants could be exchanged for tracts anywhere in the public domain. Your ancestor's warrant should show the name of the veteran, date the warrant was issued, and the name of heir or assignee (if appropriate). Some of these reflect tract location. Related papers sometimes show the names of heirs, their relationship to the veteran, and their residences. If your ancestor exchanged his warrant for a scrip certificate, his application file includes the surrendered bounty-land warrant, power of attorney, assignment, affidavit of relationship, and related correspondence.

Maybe your ancestor obtained land from another government that later came under the sovereignty of the United States. A surprising number of people acquired land this way. Before the United States obtained the area of West Florida and the lower sections of Alabama and Mississippi, settlers had obtained land grants from French, Spanish, or British governments. Private claims for this land were examined by a board of commissioners for the United States. When the commissioners' work was terminated, the uncompleted work was turned over to regular federal agencies dealing with land matters or to the courts.

Records of private land claims in the National Archives relate to land in parts of the following states: Alabama, Arizona, Arkansas, California, Colorado, Florida, Illinois, Indiana, Iowa, Louisiana, Michigan, Mississippi, Missouri, New Mexico, and Wisconsin. If your ancestor had a private land claim, the related sources to the claim may be of further value.

A numerical series without regard to type of entry was begun on 1 July 1908. Your family member's file would show the name, place of residence, tract description, patent date, and file number (which coincides with the patent record file).

Basic Procedure

Although the use of land entry records for your ancestral search is rather complex, you can learn a great deal by careful reading of detailed introductions and by interviews with qualified archivists or genealogical consultants. You should start with the tract location indicated in the county deed records and plat books and work back to the earliest named grantee of that land. If the tract location is known, you may search in the National Records Center, 4205 Suitland Road, Suitland, MD 20409.

If your ancestor patented land after 30 June 1908, use the index for the Numerical Series. You should examine the card index if he was entitled to patent before that date. If he received a land patent in Ohio through a district land office from 1800 to 1820, examine the book index of these records. If he patented land in the Virginia or the U.S. Military Districts of Ohio, see the consolidated bounty land warrant card index and auxiliary index records.

If you encounter difficulty, try to determine the approximate date of the patent and the location of the tract. Then you can search the chronologically arranged entries in an abstract book in the National Archives for the appropriate land office. Remember also that some district and general land office records have been acquired by state archives, research libraries, and private collections. Considerable amounts of other land entry information from non-governmental depositories may be identified in the volumes compiled and edited by Clifford Neal Smith: *Federal Land Series: A Calendar of Archival Materials on Patents Issued by the United States Government, with Subject, Tract and Name Indexes.* Volumes 1 and 2 were issued by the American Library Association; additional volumes will follow.

The volumes are an indispensable research guide to various archival material related to United States land patents. The first two volumes relate to patents in Ohio. Succeeding volumes will cover many other states. Federal bounty-land warrants actually submitted for patenting the land in the Military District of Ohio, and warrants exchanged for scrip, are included in the first two volumes, along with related communications with the General Land Office at Washington, D.C.

Excellent features of this work are tract descriptions pinpointing the settlers' land, the date of their settlement (which leads to fellow migrants), identification of squatters, and complete land title information.

Additional Research in the National Archives

E xplore the possibilities for additional genealogical research in the abundance of records at the National Archives. Categories include: civilian personnel records, naturalizations, passenger lists, passport applications, deaths of Americans abroad, claims files, merchant seamen's records, Coast Guard service, direct tax lists, Historical Survey publications, Indian records, and District of Columbia inhabitants' records.

If your ancestor worked for the Federal Government more than sixty years ago in a branch other than the legislative branch, his record is probably in the National Archives. An application may contain information on political activity, recommendations of various officials, or biographical data.

Naturalizations

Naturalization confers the rights and obligations of citizenship on an alien; he is given the same citizen status that he would have received had he been born in the United States. During the colonial period, a British-born individual (from England, Wales, Scotland, Ireland, or a British colony) did not need to be naturalized in a British colony in America. The Germans, Dutch, French, Swedes, and others were usually naturalized by the acts of the General Assembly of the colony. But this was not necessarily valid in every colony.

After the American Revolution, your ancestors were considered citizens of the state in which they resided, rather than of the nation as a whole, until the Fourteenth Amendment was passed in 1868. States' rights attitudes of people and the localization of records may be understood from this historical perspective. It was common practice in the nineteenth century for an immigrant to sign a statement of allegiance when he landed. Sometimes the passenger list and the naturalization list were the same record. Later in the century, the various courts took care of the process of naturalization, and the records may be in any federal, state, or local court. The federal records are being centralized in the Federal Records Centers. The federal naturalization records that were kept before 1840 are on microfilm, and others will be filmed.

In 1906 Congress established the Bureau of Immigration and Naturalization (later Immigration and Naturalization Service), which provided comprehensive regulation. It also standardized the process and the recording of naturalization. If your ancestor was naturalized after 1906, he would have had to take these steps:

(1) He would have filed a petition with the service that reviewed the case.

(2) He would have filed a petition with the clerk of the court.

(3) He would have submitted to examination by an official of the service.

(4) He would have obtained a final hearing before the judge of the court and presented a recommendation from a service official.

(5) He would have taken an oath of allegiance, and then he would have received a certificate of naturalization.

Children under 16 acquired citizenship through the naturalization of their parents or by birth in this country. Between 1855 and 1922, a woman could become a citizen either by marrying a citizen or by the naturalization of her husband. The law later required the naturalization of both husband and wife to avoid marriage mills for naturalization purposes. Spouses and minor children of citizens who served in the military during World Wars I and II were more readily naturalized. Residents of Texas, Puerto Rico, and Hawaii became citizens by blanket legislation; residents of Louisiana, Florida, the Virgin Islands, and Alaska became citizens by treaty.

With some exceptions, records of naturalizations in state and local courts are still in the custody of the courts. During the 1930s, the Works Projects Administration (WPA) photocopied naturalizations from 1787 to 1906 of four New England states—Maine, New Hampshire, Massachusetts, and Rhode Island—and prepared a Soundex index of them; the material is now in the National Archives. Records of New Jersey naturalizations from 1749 to 1810 are filed at the State Archives Division in Trenton. Records of Massachusetts naturalizations from 1885 to 1931 are filed at the State Archives in Boston. Photocopying of the desired records is now permitted unless the court or custodian issues a certified copy.

Naturalization records are less accessibile than others, but centralization may come about in time. You are in luck if your ancestor acquired public land, because he had to become naturalized to receive homestead rights. If a person was at least 21 years old at the time of the 1870 census, his citizenship is indicated. The 1900 census indicates whether a person was native born or naturalized.

Remember that your ancestor may not have obtained naturalization, which is not uncommon, but any children born to him in the United States automatically became citizens. Don't expect too much from naturalization records; however, they are important in seeking proof of an ancestor's birthplace.

Passenger Lists

If you cannot locate your ancestor's naturalization records, perhaps you can locate the passenger list for the ship on which he sailed to this country. This list may give you his occupation, the arrival date, the name of the ship and its master, and the name of his country, and sometimes the more explicit locale. In the case of British subjects, the Welsh, the Irish, and the Scots were not always distinguished from the English. The origin of these immigrants was often recorded simply as Great Britain.

Many passenger lists are available at the National Archives, and microfilms have been made of lists up to 1925. Other lists contain later records; microfilming and research of the records cannot be undertaken until fifty years have passed since the latest record contained. Many of these lists will soon become available, and research will be possible. *A Bibliography of Ship Passenger Lists, 1538–1825* by Harold Lancour (published by New York Public Library) specifies those which have been published in printed form.

You can obtain good results from indexes to New York lists before 1846 and after 1897, and throughout the 19th century from indexes to Boston, Philadelphia, Baltimore, and New Orleans lists. If you can supply the name of the port, the name of the ship, and the approximate date of arrival, the National Archives will search the customs passenger lists. If you are trying to find out something about an ancestor who arrived after 1890, you may use a directory of steamship arrivals. You may find information about arrivals before 1890 by consulting newspaper notices of ship arrivals. The directories are at the National Archives, and the newspapers are located by consulting union lists of newspapers and of newspapers in microform.

Passport Applications

If your ancestor returned to the homeland for a visit, he may have obtained a passport to protect him from military draft in the homeland or for some other reason. Passports were not required until World War I, but they frequently were obtained. Passport applications for the period before 1900 may be examined at the National Archives. Those issued during the last 75 years must be sought from the Department of State Passport Office. The application may contain a personal description, the date and court of naturalization, the exact date and place of birth, the date and port of arrival, and the name of the ship.

Deaths of Americans Abroad

Deaths of Americans abroad are reported in dispatches from American consular officials. The reports usually show the name, place of former residence, date and place of death, and the name and post of the official reporting the death. More merchants, government officials, seamen, and others have died abroad than you might expect. These records are at the National Archives.

Claim Files

Claims against the Federal Government usually show the age and residence of the claimant; sometimes the names of parents, grandparents, and other personal information are noted. The files include private claims brought before the Senate or the House of Representatives, claims resulting from the quasi-war with France over neutral rights (1797–1801), and Civil War claims. Private claims brought before the Congress are listed in a series of published indexes that are available in major libraries. Claims resulting from the dispute with France and from the Civil War are each listed in published volumes. A *representative* of the claimant from the quasi-war with France would be listed in an unpublished volume at the National Archives. Your ancestor may have filed a claim of some kind, and the possibility is worth investigating.

Merchant Seamen

A considerable body of material in the National Archives relates to merchant seamen. This includes lists of Americans impressed (required to serve as seamen) by Great Britain before the War of 1812 or imprisoned during the war, 1793–1815; applications for seamen's protection certificates and related materials, 1796–1866 and 1916–1940; crew lists for vessels entering and clearing some Atlantic and Gulf of Mexico ports, 1803–1919; and shipping articles for vessels entering or clearing many ports, 1840–1938.

Even if an ancestor had no known seagoing career, he may have signed on for a trip from New York to New Orleans or to some other southern port.

Coast Guard and Revenue Cutter Service

The names of officers and crews of the Revenue Cutter Service from 1791 to 1925 and the officers of its successor, the U.S. Coast Guard, from 1915 to 1929, are recorded and placed in appropriate files; however, fragmentary records exist before 1833. Biographical information for officers is more complete, but crew members are reported with substantial detail after 1907.

Direct Tax Lists

The Federal Government imposed a direct tax on its citizens based on a valuation made 1 October 1798. The Pennsylvania lists of citizens that were taxed are at the National Archives, and they are available on microfilm at other libraries. Lists for Massachusetts (including Maine) are at the New England Historic Genealogical Society, and those for Maryland are at the Maryland Historical Society. A tiny fraction of the lists of slave owners in a portion of Burke County, Georgia, is at the Georgia Department of Archives and History. Lists for other states have not been located. These lists are useful for locating individuals and their neighbors and acquainting you with the property of the individual.

Historical Records Survey Publications

Copies of most of the publications of the Historical Records Survey (WPA) are in the National Archives, but the microfilm publications and the unpublished project material are in the state depositories (usually the state archives). The Survey inventoried county archives, federal archives in the states, state archives, municipal and town archives, church archives, vital statistics records, and some miscellaneous records. They also made some typed transcripts, and included those relating to Spanish land grants in Florida.

You can use these inventories to identify the holdings of

county courthouses between 1936 and 1943 of wills, deeds, birth and death certificates, marriage licenses, and naturalization records. There is a bibliography of the publications, but there is not a bibliography of unpublished material. Individual state depositories may have a listing of their unpublished material.

Indian Records

Many families have traditional stories which indicate that they are descended from Indian ancestry, but only a small percentage of these stories can be proven. You can examine the records concerning Indians at the National Archives. These records include lists relating to Indian removal, annuity payrolls, annual census rolls, special rolls of the Eastern Cherokees, claims of the Eastern Cherokees, estate files, and Carlisle Indian School (Pennsylvania) files. Other general records relating to Indian research are censuses and bounty-land warrant applications. There are many records relating to the Five Civilized Tribes in Oklahoma at the Federal Records Center in Fort Worth, Texas, and at the Oklahoma Historical Society; records of other tribes are in Federal Records Centers in other locations.

There are lists relating to the migration of Cherokees, Chickasaws, Choctaws, Creeks, and Seminoles, both before and after their removal to the Indian lands. Some are census lists made prior to emigration; others are muster rolls of emigrating parties. These date primarily from 1830 to 1852. Some lists include the number of persons in each family by age group and sex and the original residence of each head of the family.

Annuity payrolls record annual payments from 1848 to 1940, but they are of most use genealogically in conjunction with the annual Indian census begun in 1885. The censuses were not taken annually in some instances even though it was required. Neither the Five Civilized Tribes nor the Eastern Cherokees had annual censuses taken until 1898. The rolls include the Indian's age, sex, and relationship to the head of the family or to another Indian on the roll. School census records start in the 1870s; they list each child, his age, birthplace, and sometimes the parents' names.

Special rolls of Eastern Cherokees date intermittently from 1835 to 1924; they show the reimbursement of individual members for land and for other purposes. The claims of the Eastern Cherokees are in the court records of *Eastern Cherokees vs. United States*. The individual files contain the English name and the Indian name of the claimant, residence, date and place of birth, name and age of each brother and sister, name and place of birth of each grandparent, and name, residence, and where appropriate, date of death of each child. Sometimes they identify the claimant with persons living when some of the early rolls were made.

Estate files from 1907 to 1940 contain wills, reports on heirship, and related papers. Card indexes are in the Bureau of Indian Affairs. The files usually show the tribe, place of residence, date of death, and age at death. Heirship reports show name of spouse and date of marriage, names and dates of marriage of parents, names of brothers and sisters, and names of the children.

Carlisle Indian School files show the student's English name, Indian name, agency, Indian nation, band, home address, percentage of Indian blood, age, and date of enrollment and departure. The folder also includes other information.

Prior to 1830, few individual records were maintained on Indians. The church mission reports and government agents' records are the chief sources for Indian genealogy in the earlier period. The records at the National Archives relate primarily to the subsequent removal of the Indians from their lands and to the reservation period of Indian history. Records of the allotment period (encouraging allotments of land) are accessible through the Bureau of Indian Affairs. These include land records, registers of families, and records of the sick and injured, births, and deaths. Many records of the U.S. Court of Claims, through which much Indian litigation has passed in recent years, are in the National Records Center at Suitland, Maryland.

The reports and findings of the U. S. Indian Claims Commission, plus publications emanating from dockets of testimony submitted to the commission, are useful for documenting history and genealogy. Publications of this material on microform are available in libraries. It is advisable to utilize the major collections of Indian history and source material as well as localized collections which often neglect Indian sources.

Records of the District of Columbia

The center at Suitland, Maryland, has the records related to the District of Columbia, which is a separately administered unit of the Federal Government. These records include naturalizations, wills, administrations, guardianships, and indentures of apprenticeships. Nearly all of the earlier chapters on records at the county and state level would apply basically to research in the District of Columbia records.

The variety of records available in Washington is rather overwhelming. Basically, if you try to retrace the steps of your ancestors and then to determine what official records they may have made in the process, you will be able to work intelligently on the accumulation of information about them.

Societies and Publications

You will find genealogical and historical societies helpful. Join the historical society and the genealogical society in each state in which your ancestors resided for a generation or more. Sometimes the two interests have combined to form one society, but many states have separate organizations. Also, join the county or regional societies of history and genealogy that relate to your ancestry.

The National Genealogical Society publishes a scholarly *Quarterly* that is worth the entire cost of membership. Its book reviews are classics. For many years these reviews have been written by Milton Rubincam, noted genealogist. The articles contain excellent presentations of methodology and useful source material.

The oldest genealogical society is the New England Historic Genealogical Society, and its *Register* has long been recognized for its good scholarship. Membership entitles you to borrow by mail from its library. The Detroit Society of Genealogical Research is important to anyone with ancestry in the Midwest. Its *Magazine* also contains valuable material to aid you in pursuing your Midwestern ancestry.

A distinguished publication, independent of any society sponsorship, is TAG, *The American Genealogist.* It was started by Donald Lines Jacobus, and it is now edited by George E. McCracken with many distinguished contributing editors. It contains excellent articles on the analysis, interpretation, and creativeness in using data from original records. The Ohio Genealogical Society was the first state organization to have chapters in various counties: it correlated activities through the state society. The Illinois State Genealogical Society has made outstanding progress in the field of the historian's involvement with genealogical usage. Texas is so large that a state society has been thriving, and a great many societies have developed throughout the state. Utah has developed an excellent state society, and much activity has been generated due to the state's Mormon background. Also, the Northwest and the California areas have active societies.

Two state societies are so notable that they should be mentioned. The New York Genealogical and Biographical Society publishes an excellent periodical, *The Record,* that is well produced and edited. Some of the material relates to other states as well as to New York. The Genealogical Society of Pennsylvania has been active for many years. Its *Pennsylvania Genealogical Magazine* (formerly *Publications)* makes valuable contributions of information. The libraries of each of these societies are well supplied with books, and their manuscript collections are mines of genealogical data.

The South has not been as fortunate as the North in having well-established genealogical societies and publications. Today, the South is gaining many societies and publications. Virginia has long had a genealogical society and it has published a quarterly for some time. John Frederick Dorman has privately published an excellent journal, *The Virginia Genealogist.* Raymond B. and Sara Seth Clark have privately issued *The Maryland and Delaware Genealogist.* The North Carolina Genealogical Society issues a splendid publication entitled the *Journal.* Laurence K. Wells is the publisher of the *South Carolina Magazine of Ancestral Research;* this magazine chiefly serves the interests of upcountry South

Carolina research. Two journals serve Georgia: the privately published *Georgia Genealogical Magazine* (previously edited by Folks Huxford and now edited by Silas Emmet Lucas), and the *Georgia Genealogical Society Quarterly*.

Florida has active groups in Miami, Palm Beach, Tampa, Orlando, and Jacksonville. Since Florida's population is largely from outside the state, their interests are very diverse and not easily represented by Florida research. Alabama has a state society, Alabama Genealogical Society, Inc., which issues a publication each quarter entitled the *Magazine*. Also there are several local societies which publish good periodicals. Mississippi has several local societies, and there is a privately published journal, the *Mississippi Genealogical Exchange*.

Kentucky Ancestors is issued by the Kentucky Historical Society. The Tennessee Genealogical Society publishes *Ansearchin' News*. Since there are three regions within the state of Tennessee, a diversity of interests is created. Louisiana has been fortunate in having two journals, the *Louisiana Genealogical Register* and the *New Orleans Genesis*. *Arkansas Family Historian* has contributed to resources for research of that state, and *Oklahoma Genealogical Society Quarterly* has been a mainstay for "the Sooners." The list is endless but we can cite another useful publication, *St. Louis Genealogical Society Quarterly*.

With so many publications, it is suggested that you pinpoint the articles you wish to peruse which deal with your people and the places where they lived. Most publications are carefully indexed in the *Genealogical Periodical Annual Index*. Here all articles that deal with a given subject are cited, and you may refer to them in genealogical libraries.

You will eventually determine your ethnic background, and then you should join the appropriate historical societies. Some of the older societies are the Pennsylvania-German Society, and the American-Jewish Historical Society.

You will determine the church affiliations of your ancestors. The historical societies of these churches can be beneficial to your research. A prominent organization of this type is the Presbyterian Historical Society in Philadelphia.

A directory of these historical societies is published by the American Association for State and Local History in Nashville, Tennessee. The membership and the activities of the particular societies are noted. A specialized directory of genealogical societies and their publications has been issued by Mary K. Meyer of Baltimore.

Lineage and Patriotic Societies

Ancestral research is sometimes equated with the activities of a society whose members descend from a specific category of persons. This is quite erroneous, for the member may have little genealogical interest other than to gain proof of descent to qualify himself for membership. Professional genealogists or experienced amateurs often assist those desiring to get their papers prepared for membership.

These societies based on lineage, sometimes called patriotic or hereditary societies, vary widely in their characteristics. Virtually everyone knows of the Daughters of the American Revolution; this organization has a large membership and supports an outstanding library. A comprehensive listing of these societies may be found in the *Hereditary Register of the United States of America*.

The oldest society, founded in 1637, is the Ancient and Honorable Artillery Company of Massachusetts. It maintains a military museum and library at the historic Fanueil Hall in Boston. Membership is no longer confined to lineage from those who served prior to 1738.

Here is a representative list, by no means complete, of the types of lineage societies; membership is drawn from persons who are descendants from specific categories of forebears:

Members of military units of Colonial America
    Jersey Blues
National origins
    Dutch—Holland Society of New York
Service in the Patriot cause
    Daughters of the American Revolution
Colonial officials
    National Society of Colonial Dames of America
Passengers on earliest ship to a given colony
    General Society of Mayflower Descendants
Virginia founding settlers
    Order of First Families of Virginia
Magna Carta barons
    National Society, Daughters of the Barons of Runnemede
Colonial clergy
    Society for the Descendants of the Colonial Clergy
Confederate veterans
    United Daughters of the Confederacy
Illegitimate children of British kings
    Descendants of the Illegitimate Sons and Daughters of
        the Kings of Britain
Tavern keepers of the colonial period
    Descendants of Colonial Tavern Keepers (Flagon and
        Trencher)
Texas service prior to annexation
    Daughters of the Republic of Texas
State or city pioneers
    Louisiana Colonials

Anyone with the slightest knowledge of these societies is aware of the number and variety of lineage organizations which are not included in the above sampling.

Analyze, Interpret, and Correlate
Your Information

Accurate genealogy is based upon facts, which you can prove. Accuracy demands being alert to each clue as a detective searching for each element of a case. You must have competent evidence to prove your facts, as an attorney who must present his case in a court of law. You have to correlate information from many sources and then show the validity of your conclusions.

Thus, it is necessary to refer to all sources (author, title, publisher, date, volume, page) and persons interviewed (name, address, age, relationship to the individual or to the topic). And it is necessary to have a knowledge of the history, geography, and social customs of the area and people you are researching. Some knowledge of the history of the law and the language of the area and the people is necessary to understand your facts.

It is essential to assemble all records which pertain to your ancestry, including court records, personal records, and census records.

First, arrange the material you have in chronological order, and then arrange it by name or place. Review of your material may disclose any cases of implausible circumstances, such as births of children after the mother has reached the age of 50, or death of an individual beyond the age of 100.

Land records as well as probate records may be required to clarify or establish family relationships. Proof by land records is usually incontrovertible. Land and personal tax lists and powers of attorney are often required to prove facts.

Migration patterns are reflected in the land records. It is possible your ancestors could have followed a migration pattern. If so, a majority of persons who settled the same new area would have migrated from the same place. Thus, examination of pertinent records of both locations is suggested.

Acknowledgment by the grantor of a deed provides evidence that the person was present at the location on that date, regardless of when the deed was recorded. Acquisition of property in a new location shortly after conveyance of previous property may develop a chain of evidence to support genealogical reconstruction of your family's history.

Court minutes or orders reveal the appointment of guardians for minors and estate administrators. These records sometimes include acknowledgment in court of minors who attain legal age. These are often neglected in family research.

Under the British common law during the colonial period, the estate could not be divided until the youngest child became of age. Thus, chancery court records provide evidence of attainment of legal age. Suits were filed on behalf of the minor children naming the other children as defendants. A minor child would first appear in the list of plaintiffs, until he attained legal age. He would later appear in the list of defendants in subsequent actions if he had had siblings who were still minors. The history of such a case divulges much family history through proper analysis.

Since white males were taxable at age 16 (in many jurisdictions), their names on tax lists indicate attainment of age. Because of the law of primogeniture, whereby the entire real property of the father passed to the eldest son at the death of the father, there are instances in which the eldest son is not even mentioned in the will because the father knew that he would receive the property by law. Thus you cannot assume that every child is mentioned in the will in the colonial period (primogeniture was eliminated by law at various dates, chiefly in the 1780s). Similarly, absence of an eldest daughter in a will may be explained by an examination of the land records; the father may have given or sold her a portion of the land for a nominal price at her marriage.

An instructive example of analysis of records may be found in an article, "Two William Persons of Virginia: Some Corrections of Walker's Persons Lineage," by Virginia P. Livingston, in *The Virginia Genealogist*, October 1967.

Census records are notoriously inaccurate, particularly in recording the ages of adults. A succession of census records containing the entries of the family must be examined to reveal the likely age. Birthplaces may not be indicated accurately since they are frequently representative of the childhood residence but not necessarily the birthplace.

Newspaper obituary accounts are based on information from persons who may not have precise information about the deceased. These accounts may be used as clues to obtain other data.

Persons of the same name in the same locale require careful research to eliminate each one from consideration. This is necessary to prove that your ancestor is the *only* person in Granville County, North Carolina, who could have been related to you.

Beware of obvious conclusion. One devout Baptist couple was married by a Methodist clergyman in a lawn ceremony instead of the customary church wedding. The ceremony took place one thousand miles away from the homes of the couple. The groom was on leave during the war, and they moved within three days to an adjoining state to establish their first residence. You may not be aware of circumstances that happened at a particular time, and therefore you must piece together information.

Several procedures for verifying facts regarding ancestral histories are presented in a booklet, *Is That Lineage Right?*, issued by the National Society, Daughters of the American Revolution (The Society, 1965). Mastery of this verification procedure will assure you of the validity of your ancestral research or reveal matters which need correction or substantiation.

Overseas Ancestry

If you have proof of the immigration of an ancestor, you may be anxious to "get your feet wet" by crossing the water. However, you must complete your research in this country *before* you travel to other countries. You must be absolutely sure you have examined all of the data necessary to pinpoint your ancestor's home abroad.

Have you read the articles in historical and genealogical periodicals that pertain to the surname you are researching? Have you read the articles which pertain to an ancestor's geographical area overseas? In other words, have you exhausted the possible sources in this country that pertain to your ancestor?

If you have established the certainty of your lineage back to the immigrant, then you may consider the extent of the research problem overseas. What was the population of your ancestor's country at the time he migrated? Was he one person in only 100,000 people residing there, or was he one in 2 million? If you know this fact, you will comprehend the extent of your overseas research better.

Is your ancestor's surname a common one in that country? Or is the surname unusual enough to limit your search to a tiny segment of the population? Can you find a report (perhaps under government auspices) of the incidence of surnames, perhaps within a county, principality, or governmental subdivision? Knowledge of these factors will help to define the extent of research needed.

Now what do you do? It is necessary to have or to obtain sufficient knowledge of the country's history to understand the influences on your ancestors' lives. Without this knowledge, you can't perceive the causes and effects that influenced their lives and affected the genealogical data you seek. You will need to know the history of the localized area in which your ancestors lived. This calls for more background reading at major academic and research libraries. Journals may be harder to locate, but you must examine them for every shred of information.

A reading knowledge of the language(s) is necessary for the research. The alternative to this procedure of developing the historical background of your ancestors is to employ the services of a thoroughly dependable genealogist who is experienced in exploring the records of the area. Only advanced genealogists of impeccable reputation should be considered. The Board for Certification of Genealogists is responsible for certification in this professional field, but it does not certify persons dealing with overseas ancestry. However, a certified genealogist in this country may have a colleague overseas who is capable of assisting you.

In England there is an Association of Genealogists and Record Agents which will inform you of qualified persons to contact for specific geographic areas. Similar organizations may have been formed on the continent of Europe. In lieu of such assistance, it might be advisable to contact the appropriate archivists and the librarians of major libraries in that country in which you are interested.

Study carefully the pertinent chapters in *Genealogical Research* volumes 1 and 2 published by the American Society of Genealogists. These works provide specific information and are considered standard manuals for professional work.

They may be supplemented by other sources in major libraries.

Heraldry

Technically, heraldry encompasses the art and office of heralds—those people who officially record genealogies and marshal coronations and other ceremonies.

However, a second and more popular interpretation of the term refers to coats of arms, or "armory." *Burke's General Armory* (and its supplement by Humphrey-Smith) is a standard work for the British Isles. Rietstap's *Armorial Général* is the standard European work. But it is a serious mistake to "adopt" any coat of arms from these volumes.

The term *coat of arms* is derived from the surcoat which was worn over the armor. It was made of linen for ordinary wear, and of silk for tournaments and other special occasions. A shield bore the same design. Since arms can and do exist without crests, it is regrettable that the whole design is sometimes erroneously called a crest.

The descriptions of arms are in old French, which was used throughout much of western Europe as the common language of the ruling class in the Middle Ages. Armorial descriptions are a kind of shorthand, briefly describing in words the design elements and arrangement. We will not attempt to discuss the subject since it is basically not a part of genealogy.

Entitlement to arms was looked upon as a privilege, so rulers were quick to assume control of the granting of arms. For instance, in England, the College of Arms is empowered to grant arms, and heralds hold office by appointment of the crown. It was not established by Parliament nor does it have authority from Parliament.

In Scotland a different method of granting arms is used. Since 1672, Parliament has granted the successive Lords

Lyon the power to stipulate the exact design of arms. At maturity, each Scot is expected to matriculate his arms in the Lyon Office. In turn, the office alters his arms to differentiate them from arms of other members of the family.

However, when pursuing your ancestry in any country, it is a mistake to assume that your family's supposed right to a coat of arms was granted for services to the state. It is more likely that if your ancestor was "armigerous," he simply reached a certain social grade and assumed or was granted a coat of arms befitting his rise in social level.

A common misunderstanding is that every family of respectable social standing must have a coat of arms somewhere. Actually, prominent families may come from humble immigrants, and a laborer may be a descendent of a family of prominence.

A most lucrative racket has been built on the common assumption that a person's name indicates a relationship with other families of the same name. However, the names Woodman and Smith are examples of names given to people in many locations and derived from the occupations of the time. Even if your name is unusual and is found in only one small locality, you cannot assume a relationship among all who bear the name. It is necessary to prove your male line of descent from someone who is legally entitled to a coat of arms. The right to a coat of arms is property, and its descent from one generation to another must be proved. Descent from a specific arms-bearing family is essential before you can use that family's arms.

The Committee of Heraldry of the New England Historic Genealogical Society carefully examines proofs submitted by interested persons. They have published successive parts of a continuing Roll of Arms for the benefit of those who desire authentication of their arms. The committee has no government authority but it provides a sort of imprimatur on your genealogical proof of right to arms.

Completing Your Family History

You have come a long way from the point where you began research on your family history. You have learned that it is important to verify and prove every statement. You also know it is important to note the exact source of each item of data. Now it is time to put it all together in a story that relates your family history.

Tell your history simply and straightforwardly. Don't embellish it with imaginative tales of heroic conduct. Don't suppress or misrepresent the truth, but you need not spotlight the family's gray areas, either. Be honest with yourself and with your readers. After all, your history will not be read by many who are not within the family.

You will probably want to have a capable editor review your history after it has been completed. Don't think that your writing will not require revision. Authors seldom can edit their own work adequately. Family historians tend to assume the reader knows things about the history that he really does not know. Be prepared for the shock of seeing much of your work questioned without mercy. You must revise your book to make it better.

Unless you have clear proof of your overseas ancestry, do not include it. If the family tradition has been strengthened by some initial research overseas, you may mention it. Admit your lack of proof, and label the tradition for what it is; state your supportive material or information.

Don't publish a coat of arms in your book unless your right to that arms has been verified by competent genealogical research. It is preferable to publish a good photograph of the colonial homestead, of the ship on which your ancestor arrived, or of a particularly interesting document. Be sure the document is legible since a document must be readable after it is photographically reduced for publication. Don't include a document that is commonly available such as a land patent. Perhaps a photograph of a four or five generation group would be a good choice. It is wise to include as many photographs of people, places, and documents as you can. The test is whether your book will be of genuine interest to your readers. Some advice from a capable genealogist or a good editor may be well worth the small fee you have to pay.

Now to the history. Start with your earliest known ancestors and write out their story in full. Then relate the story of each of their children giving the account in full for each child from birth to death. Proceed chronologically through the generations. Your chapters will vary in length, because you will know more about some members of your family than others.

The manuscript should be typed on 8½″ by 11″ white paper and double-spaced. Leave good margins around the page. Dates are expressed under the system generally used by genealogists: 13 August 1975.

Talk with a reputable printer who has published books equal in size to the one you contemplate. Ask him about capitalization, punctuation, and uniform treatment of figures. If he advises printing directly from typewriter composition, you will need his advice about margins, spacing, and typeface. If you have a lengthy manuscript, you may want to get several bids on the book before you begin the final typing. Examine book samples that please you.

When you take your finished manuscript to the printer, obtain a signed agreement from him on the number of printed and bound books that you want, an exact sample of the paper to be used, and the delivery date of the books. Turn the typed manuscript over to him, and do not make any further changes. Changes in the final manuscript are very costly.

Unless you have an unusually large family and extensive correspondence with many people interested in the family, it is advisable to print 200 or 300 copies. Your rosy expectations of book sales will not be realized, and you should save your money.

While the printer is manufacturing the book, you can spend your time promoting it. You may want to write the relatives with whom you corresponded while researching the family. Tell them the book is going to be available at a specified date (somewhat later than the date promised by the printer, because you will encounter delays). Perhaps you can time the book to be available for Christmas buying or a family reunion. A family history makes an excellent gift for relatives.

A very simple one-page announcement of the book's availability can be prepared and inexpensively reproduced by a printer or a lettershop. Be sure to include your name and address, the publication date, details about the number of pages, number of illustrations (photographs), and any other pertinent listing of the families included and geographic areas covered. Mail the announcement to all of your correspondents; send one to *Genealogical Books in Print*, 6818 Lois Drive, Springhill, VA 22150, and have your book listed in the next edition of that publication. Save the list, and repeat the mailing at least once.

If your book is being printed directly from the typed copy, you will have to prepare the index before the manuscript is given to the printer. If type is being set from the manuscript, then you cannot prepare the index until the page proofs of the type are completed. Much detail is required to prepare the index to a large book, but if you can handle it, you should prepare the index yourself.

Here's a relatively simple way to do it. Mark each name on a copy of the finished pages, and have punched cards made for each entry with the appropriate page number. These cards can be sorted manually or by computer very quickly. Then a printout of the card entries can be obtained and edited to remove duplications, and the type can be composed for the index pages. Another method is to write the name and page number on adding machine tape. Cut them apart, sort into paper cups, having one for each letter of the alphabet. Then alphabetize the slips in each cup, working with one letter at a time. Then the index is ready to be typed in alphabetical order. Remember, a book of family history is *valueless* without an index.

When the books are completed, you need to know about sales taxes. Get competent advice from your accountant on how to handle this; you may want to pay the tax on the manufacturing cost (the printer's invoice).

When you try to sell the book, remember these points: Insist that orders be prepaid with satisfaction guaranteed. Don't send the book on approval to anyone. However, libraries and institutions are exceptions, and will have to be billed. Review copies should be sent to the *National Genealogical Society Quarterly*, and to a regional genealogical magazine. Also, send copies to the appropriate genealogical magazines in states where your family has located.

Store your copies in a warm, dry place away from moisture, insects and rodents.

Genealogical Scholarship

Historically, the quality of genealogical research varies greatly, ranging from utter foolishness to remarkable scholarship. Genealogy began centuries ago, primarily to legitimize the succession of kings, princes, and priests. The laws of inheritance governing the descent of real estate have relied upon accurate genealogical data. The privileges of the aristocracy were largely based on genealogical claims, some of which were doubtful or downright spurious.

Now there is worldwide interest in the genealogies of people in all walks of life. Thousands of people are researching their family histories and trying to link with a famous or noble personage. However, this trend is diminishing, and a more enlightened climate is developing. More people are seriously tracing their ancestry without any preconceived notion of elite forebears.

In England, individuals who are devoted to the study of local history, archaeology, biography, and genealogy are called antiquarians; it is a highly respected term. In the United States, this term usually refers to an amateur local historian, one who is a mere sampler of bits and pieces of history. We need to adopt the true meaning of an antiquarian. Genealogists should acquire a broad knowledge and depth of local history to appreciate and understand the records they are researching.

Individuals in many professions may benefit from the knowledge a genealogist acquires. Attorneys sometimes use genealogical research to settle family estates. Biographers may use genealogical methods to develop the family background. Librarians need to be familiar with the archival sources for adequate reference service to the readers. Medical research scientists, especially geneticists, can benefit from genealogical principles; they can use them to determine the validity of the pedigrees from which data are extracted. Historians may also benefit from the genealogist's knowledge of family relationships to interpret the broader dimensions of history.

Genealogical scholarship is dependent on knowledge of the sources (the bibliography), on awareness of the bearing of events and movements on individuals, on analytic power to see solutions to a problem, on detective instinct to follow a good lead, on perseverance to work on a knotty problem with meager results, and on internal joy in the discovery of any helpful information.

The critical spirit that has ridiculed careless historians and dishonest pedigree-makers began largely with J. Horace Round, an eminent English medievalist. Round poured scorn on those who fabricated pedigrees or accepted uncritically the statements and claims of ancient lineage. His blistering attacks brought him no popularity even among scholars, but they established a new respect for the advanced discipline of genealogy. While not the first to demand proof of a pedigree for every generation, he was the standard bearer for respectable history and genealogy.

He was followed by Oswald Barron and G. E. Cokayne, and in America by Dr. Arthur Adams and Donald Lines Jacobus. From these roots, the contemporary class of genealogists has evolved and demanded critical standards in scholarship.

In turn, the National Genealogical Society has acquired more competent leadership. The American Society of Genealogists has honored genealogical writers. Also, the Latter Day Saints have begun to practice better standards of genealogical scholarship. Archives and libraries are beginning to recognize a need for competent genealogical personnel.

Meredith B. Colket, Jr., formerly at the National Archives, now at the Western Reserve Historical Society, and Dr. Ernest Posner, of American University, and former archivist in Berlin, collaborated in planning a course begun at the National Archives in 1950. Dr. Jean Stephenson succeeded Mr. Colket as the director for several years. Respected genealogical practices were taught in this course, and this led to more intelligent use of the archival resources.

Milton Rubincam was the first invited lecturer at the 1962 inaugural Institute at Samford University in Birmingham, Alabama, and he has been the mainstay of the program. In 1965, Samford University assumed administration of the Institute, and the author became the Director. It later became the Institute of Genealogy and Historical Research. Dr. Jean Stephenson, long considered the dean of American genealogists, taught for several years at the Institute. Virginia P. Livingston, a specialist in southern genealogy; John I. Coddington, an authority on New England genealogy and migrations; and Kenn Stryker-Rodda, an authority on Dutch settlements in New York and New Jersey and an academician interested in genealogical education and methodology, have all contributed immeasurably to this Institute. It is now cosponsored by the Board for Certification of Genealogists and Samford University.

Brigham Young University in Utah offers a two-year associate degree in genealogy. Courses in genealogy are also offered at Ricks College in Rexburg, Idaho.

Many colleges, junior colleges, and adult education programs are offering brief courses in the fundamentals of genealogy. Some of these emphasize the hobbyist approach to the subject, while others perceive and emphasize the scholarly requirements. Library schools, archival curricula, and graduate history departments are offering courses for genealogical research.

Genealogical societies are offering workshops, some of which feature highly respected genealogists. These workshops provide opportunities for basic genealogical instruction for thousands who cannot enroll at an academic institute for a regular course.

Certification

There has always been a need to establish standards of ethics and practices for professional genealogists. In the past, anyone could set up a genealogical practice. There was no organization to determine the validity of his credentials. A person desiring to employ the services of a competent researcher had no standards by which to determine his ability. Unqualified individuals could offer their services, and little could be done to stop them.

In 1964, the Board for Certification of Genealogists was created in Washington, D. C., and certification became available. Three types of certification were established. A *Certified Genealogist* (C.G.) is qualified to compile a family history or to construct a pedigree which is based on primary sources (original records). He must know the principles of genealogical research and apply this knowledge to each problem as it develops. He must be able to select the best evidence and to draw logical conclusions. He must have a substantial knowledge of genealogical and historical bibliography, particularly the history, bibliography, and records of the areas in which he specializes. He must be able to prepare family histories that are satisfactorily planned, arranged, and documented. He also must be able to prepare an intelligent and businesslike report on the pedigree or to complete an application for lineage society membership with the appropriate, full evidence.

A *Certified American Lineage Specialist* (C.A.L.S.) prepares papers for applicants seeking admission to lineage societies. He must be able to prepare papers that are supported by evidence to prove the family connection generation by generation. He must know the types of records applicable to his purpose, how to locate them, and how to interpret them. He must base his papers on the best evidence available to substantiate the pedigree; he may not rely on compendia or family histories. He should obtain authentic copies of supporting documents and attach them to the paper. If these are unobtainable, he should obtain the abstracts that he needs. The specialist may not depend on the papers of other applicants that have been accepted by societies, since earlier papers may have been derived from erroneous information.

A *Genealogical Record Searcher* (G.R.S.) examines records to determine if information of genealogical, historical, or biographical value is available, and reports the results of the search. He must be well informed as to the records available in the localities where he works. He must know the purpose and meaning of the records, how to locate them, and how to read and interpret them. He must know how to prepare a complete abstract, stating the correct meaning of the document and giving the facts in the correct form. He must be able to prepare an intelligent, businesslike report of the results of his search.

To become certified, an individual must submit his completed work as a demonstration of his competence in the type of certification applied for. After careful scrutiny by three separate judges, the applicant may be certified if he subscribes to a code of ethics. The code basically requires that a certified individual give his clients competent, honorable, prompt, and fair treatment.

Charlatans and Thieves

The study of ancestry has been plagued with those who are unwilling to require accuracy in their research. Many have accepted improper or unproved links with a person of noble birth as fact. Thus charlatans and thieves have practiced successful schemes to bilk the gullible public.

A scheme that has met with success and profit has been the "missing heir" racket. Although this scheme is probably less commonly practiced than fifty years ago, it still victimizes many. Persons purporting to represent interests in an inheritance have claimed that the inheritance has been tied up for some time due to lack of contact with missing heirs. They entice people, even of modest means, to employ them to seek the legacy. They take the client on many so-called research visits and overseas conferences; these are supposedly designed to establish the client's right to the inheritance. After the client's funds are depleted, the case is declared hopeless and the client is left financially drained.

Another form of profit making which is dubious is the practice of some concerns to offer a report or a booklet to the public. The report is a mere compilation of surname extracts from censuses, county histories, compendia, and random sources. Such a compilation is of little value, and hardly deserves its name. The buyer gets much less than he expected, but the advertising is carefully worded to prevent legal action.

Another misleading practice is to establish a business under the name of an organization that is similar to a well-known professional organization and to advertise professional services. The buyer gets less than he pays for, and the genuine professional organization is burdened with the task of taking any legal action necessary to force the business to change its name.

In recent years, organizations have sprung up in Washington and Utah which employ questionable schemes. Some of these offer to provide workshops for local genealogical and historical societies at no charge. Assuming that the offer emanates from a respectable organization, the local genealogical society does not suspect anything amiss and sometimes proceeds with the plans to have a workshop. The workshop turns out to be primarily a high-pressure sales campaign designed to sell expensive, over-priced literature. This information may already be readily available in genealogical manuals and treatises. The information is usually reworded to circumvent the copyright laws.

As with so many popular interests, there are unethical practitioners and unscrupulous enterprisers among the honest practitioners. The serious person interested in his proper family history will avoid these traps and will discipline himself to a competent search.

Afterword

If, after all this, you cannot leave the family history alone for some time, then you have probably contracted a common malady known as "Geneosis" (Helmboldese). The symptoms are early rising (for a prompt start on research), shortened lunches (for maximum time at archives, courthouse, or library), attentiveness to the mail (to peruse some long-awaited book or family record), and eagerness to travel (for research and family visits).

People who become interested in family history are usually alert and fascinating. The majority of these individuals are wonderful persons with a zest for life. It seems to me that they live longer than others, probably because they have a reason for living and goals to achieve. Of human interests, I can think of none better.

Bibliography

BASIC GENEALOGICAL RESEARCH

Colket, Meredith B., Jr. *Creating a Worthwhile Family Genealogy.* Reprint. Washington, DC: National Genealogical Society, 1968.
Sound and concise discussion.

Doane, Gilbert H. *Searching for Your Ancestors: The How and Why of Genealogy.* 4th ed. Minneapolis: University of Minnesota Press, 1973.
Instructive, often humorous account of genealogical research methods and sources (especially applicable to New England). Also available in paperback.

Jaussi, Laureen Richardson, and Gloria Duncan Chaston. *Fundamentals of Genealogical Research.* Salt Lake City: Deseret Book Co., 1972.
Primarily intended for Latter Day Saints researchers.

Williams, Ethel W. *Know Your Ancestors: A Guide to Genealogical Research.* Rutland, VT: Charles E. Tuttle Co., 1960.
A basic text, particularly applicable to northern United States research.

Wright, Norman E. *Building an American Pedigree: A Study in Genealogy.* Provo, UT: Brigham Young University Press, 1974.
Comprehensive work, incorporating thorough explanation and illustrations of greatly varied record sources.

Zabriskie, George O. *Climbing Our Family Tree Systematically.* Salt Lake City: Parliament Press, 1969.
Emphasizes systematic investigation, careful planning of research campaigns, and reasoning for genealogical accuracy.

BIBLIOGRAPHIES

Filby, P. William. *American & British Genealogy & Heraldry: A Selected List of Books.* 1970. 2nd ed. Chicago: American Library Association, 1975.

Rubincam, Milton. *Genealogy: A Selected Bibliography.* 3rd rev. ed. Prepared for the Institute of Genealogy and Historical Research, Samford University. Birmingham, AL: Banner Press, 1974.

Schreiner-Yantis, Netti, ed. *Genealogical Books in Print.* Springfield, VA: Privately published, 1975.

MANUALS & REFERENCE WORKS

Daughters of the American Revolution. *Is That Lineage Right?* Washington, DC: Daughters of the American Revolution, 1958.
Valuable for aid in checking statements in lineages, difficult problems regarding names, shifting state and county lines, calendar changes.

Everton, George B., Sr. *A Handy Book for Genealogists.* 6th ed. Salt Lake City: Deseret Book Co., 1971.
Contains lists of printed census records, genealogist's checklist of Historical Records Survey publications, maps showing counties of each state and counties of bordering states.

Greenwood, Val D. *The Researcher's Guide to American Genealogy.* Introduction by Milton Rubincam. Baltimore, MD: Genealogical Publishing Co., 1973.
Identifies and classifies the various types of records used in genealogical research, gives historical and legal background, groups them in convenient tables, explains their uses.

Stevenson, Noel C. *Search and Research: the Researcher's Handbook. A Guide to Official Records and Library Sources for Investigators, Historians, Genealogists, Lawyers, and Librarians.* Rev. ed. Salt Lake City: Deseret Book Co., 1973.
Valuable reference work: lists libraries, historical and genealogical societies, and archives; specifies court records, military rosters, rolls, and records, Federal and state censuses, official records, etc.

ADVANCED & SPECIALIZED WORKS

Harland, Derek, *Genealogical Research Standards.* Salt Lake City: Bookcraft, 1963.
Describes in detail the steps of a research campaign.

Jacobus, Donald Lines. *Genealogy as Pastime and Profession.* 2nd rev. ed. Introduction by Milton Rubincam. Baltimore, MD: Genealogical Publishing Co., 1971.

First published in 1930, brought completely up to date by the distinguished author, who died in 1970. Classic in genealogical books.

Kirkham, E. Kay. *Professional Techniques and Tactics in American Genealogical Research*. Logan, UT: Everton Publishers, 1973.

Provides advice for the person desiring to take up genealogical research as a profession.

National Genealogical Society. *General Aids to Genealogical Research*. National Genealogical Society Special Publication No. 14. Washington, DC: National Genealogical Society, 1957.

Selected articles from NGSQ dealing with pitfalls, scholarship, county atlases, territorial papers, Quaker records, Pennsylvania county records, German Reformed Church records in Pennsylvania, Scwenkfelder records, Pennsylvania research.

Rubincam, Milton and Jean Stephenson, ed. *Genealogical Research Methods and Sources* 1. Washington, DC: American Society of Genealogists, 1960.

Discusses general principles of research, source materials, research in the 13 original states and Europe, heraldry, surnames, legal aspects of genealogy, etc.

Stevenson, Noel C. *The Genealogical Reader*. Salt Lake City: Deseret Book Co., 1958.

Anthology of genealogical articles; covers such subjects as pitfalls, the calendar, heraldry, tradition and family history, royal ancestry, probate law and custom, marriage, interpreting genealogical records, fraudulent pedigrees, etc.

Stryker-Rodda, Kenn, ed. *Genealogical Research* 2. Washington, DC: American Society of Genealogists, 1971.

Discusses migrations into the Northwest territory, research in states east of the Mississippi River (not covered in the first volume), migrations to Ontario and genealogical sources therein, and Huguenot and Jewish migrations.

INDEXES TO PEDIGREES & HISTORIES

Crowther, G. Rodney III. *Surname Index to Sixty-Five Volumes of Colonial and Revolutionary Pedigrees*. Foreword by Milton Rubincam. Washington, DC: National Genealogical Society Special Publication No. 27, 1964.

Glenn, Thomas Allen. *A List of Some American Genealogies Which Have Been Printed in Book Form*. 1897. Reprint. Baltimore: Genealogical Publishing Co., 1969.

Jacobus, Donald Lines. *My Own Index.* Index to Genealogical Periodicals, vol. 3. New Haven: Privately published, 1953.

Kaminkow, Marion J. *Genealogies in the Library of Congress: A Bibliography.* 2 vols. Baltimore, MD: Magna Carta Book Co., 1972.

Marshall, George W. *The Genealogist's Guide.* (British pedigrees) Introduction by Anthony J. Camp. Baltimore, MD: Genealogical Publishing Co., 1967.

Munsells' Sons, Joel. *Index to American Genealogies* and *Supplement 1900 to 1908.* Reprint. Baltimore, MD: Genealogical Publishing Co., 1967.

Rider, Fremont, ed. and comp. *American Genealogical-Biographical Index.* Vols.–93 complete (Jones, Emma to Jundre) Middletown, CT: Godfrey Memorial Library, 1952–.

Whitmore, John B. *A Genealogical Guide: An Index to British Pedigrees in Continuation of Marshall's Genealogists' Guide.* Reprint. London: Society of Genealogists, 1953.

INDEXES TO PERIODICALS

These works are listed in the order in which the researcher should use them.

Munsell's Sons, Joel. *List of Titles of Genealogical Articles in American Periodicals and Kindred Works.* Albany, NY: J. Munsell's Sons, 1899.

Jacobus, Donald Lines. *Index to Genealogical Periodicals.* Reprint (3 vols. in 1). Baltimore, MD: Genealogical Publishing Co., 1973.

New-England Historical and Genealogical Register Index. Vols. 1–50. Reprint. (4 vols.). Baltimore, MD: Genealogical Publishing Co., 1972.

The New England Historical and Genealogical Register Index (Abridged) to vols. *51–112.* (1897–1958). Marlborough, MA: Privately published, 1959.

Fisher, Carleton E. *Topical Index to the National Genealogical Society Quarterly Vols. 1–50* (1912–1962). NGS Special Publication No. 29, Washington, DC: National Genealogical Society, 1964.

Waldenmaier, Inez. *Annual Index to Genealogical Periodicals and Family Histories, 1956–1962.* Washington, DC: Privately published, 1962.

Genealogical Periodical Annual Index. 1962–1965 compiled by Ellen Stanley Rogers; 1966–1973 compiled by George E. Russell; 1974–. Compiled by Laird Towle. Bowie, MD: Privately published. 1962–.

GUIDES TO RECORD SOURCES

Colket, Meredith B., Jr., and Frank E. Bridgers. *Guide to Genealogical Records in the National Archives.* Washington, DC: National Archives and Records Service, 1964.
Available from Superintendent of Documents, Government Printing Office; perhaps also from local government book store. Detailed description of major genealogical resources on the federal level.

Kirkham, E. Kay. *A Handy Guide to Record-Searching in the Larger Cities of the United States.* Logan, UT: Everton Publishers, 1974.
Concise guide to the places one goes to research.

Radoff, Morris L., Gust Skordas, Phebe R. Jacobsen. *The County Courthouses and Records of Maryland, Part II: The Records.* Annapolis, MD: Hall of Records Commission, Publication No. 13, 1963.
Part I of this work deals with courthouse architecture and history; Part II is indispensable for the genealogist of Maryland families.

Smith, Clifford Neal. *A Calendar of Archival Materials on the Land Patents Issued by the United States Government, with Subject, Tract, and Name Indexes, 1788–1810.* Federal Land Series, vol. 1. Chicago: American Library Association, 1972.

Smith, Clifford Neal. *Federal Bounty-land Warrants of the American Revolution, 1799–1835.* Federal Land Series, vol. 2. Chicago: American Library Association, 1973.
The above two are indispensable for genealogists, historians, archivists, land-title searchers, and librarians.

U.S. National Center for Health Statistics. *Where to Write for Birth & Death Records.* Washington, DC: Government Printing Office. Consult latest edition. Pamphlet listing addresses of vital records sources.

U.S. National Center for Health Statistics. *Where to Write for Divorce Records.* Washington, DC: Government Printing Office. Pamphlet listing addresses of divorce record sources.

U.S. National Center for Health Statistics. *Where to Write for Marriage Records.* Washington, DC: Government Printing Office. Consult latest edition. Pamphlet listing addresses of vital records sources.

CHURCH RECORDS

Fries, Adelaide L. "Moravian Church Records as a Source of Genealogical Material." *National Genealogical Society Quarterly* 24 (March 1936): 1–9.

Helmbold, F. Wilbur. "Baptist Records for Genealogy and History." *National Genealogical Society Quarterly* 61 (September 1973): 168–178.

Hinke, William J. "German Reformed Church Records in Pennsylvania." *National Genealogical Society Quarterly* 37 (June 1949): 34–38.

Kieffer, Elizabeth. "Genealogical Resources of the Historical Society of the Evangelical and Reformed Church." *National Genealogical Society Quarterly* 48 (September 1960): 113–126.

Kirkham, E. Kay. *A Survey of American Church Records.* Salt Lake City: Deseret Book Company, 1959.

Miller, William. *Presbyterian Records.* Salt Lake City: Genealogical Society of the Church of Jesus Christ of the Latter Day Saints, 1969.

Ness, John, Jr. *Methodist Records.* Salt Lake City: Genealogical Society of the Church of Jesus Christ of the Latter Day Saints, 1969.

Schell, Edwin. "Sources for Genealogical Research in Methodist Records." *National Genealogical Society Quarterly* 50 (December 1962): 177–182.

Schultz, Selina Girhard. "Schwenckfelder Genealogical Records." *National Genealogical Society Quarterly* 39 (June 1951): 33–37.

Shellem, Rev. John J. *Roman Catholic Sacramental Records.* Salt Lake City: Genealogical Society of the Church of Jesus Christ of the Latter Day Saints, 1969.

Spence, Thomas H., Jr. "The Genealogist and Ecclesiastical Records." *National Genealogical Society Quarterly* 47 (December 1959): 167–172.

Stern, Malcolm H. *Jewish Synagogue Records.* Salt Lake City: Genealogical Society of the Church of Jesus Christ of the Latter Day Saints, 1969.

Suelflow, Rev. August R. *Records of the Lutheran Churches of America.* Salt Lake City: Genealogical Society of the Church of Jesus Christ of the Latter Day Saints, 1969.

Tolles, Frederick B. "A New Tool for Genealogical Research: The William Wade Hinshaw Index to Quaker Meeting Records." *National Genealogical Society Quarterly* 38 (June 1950): 39–41.

Williams, Ethel W. "Quaker Records." *Know Your Ancestors.* Rutland, VT: Charles E. Tuttle Co., 1974.

SPECIAL TOPICS—HANDWRITING

Kirkham, E. Kay. *How to Read the Handwriting and Records of Early America.* Salt Lake City: Kay Publishing Co., 1965.

SPECIAL TOPICS—HERALDRY

Burke, Sir John Bernard. *The General Armory of England, Scotland, Ireland and Wales; Comprising a Registry of Armorial Bearings from the Earliest to the Prese.it Time.* 1884. Reprint. Baltimore, MD: Genealogical Publishing Co., 1969.

Fox-Davies, Arthur Charles. *A Complete Guide to Heraldry.* Revised and annotated by J. P. Brooke-Little. London: Thomas Nelson and Sons, 1969.

Rietstap, Johannes Baptist. *Armorial Général.* 2 vols. Baltimore, MD: Heraldic Book Co., 1965.

Rolland, V. and H. V. *Supplement to the Armorial Général by J. B. Rietstap.* 6 vols. Baltimore, MD: Genealogical Publishing Co., 1969–70.

Stephenson, Jean. *Heraldry for the American Genealogist.* Washington, DC: National Genealogical Society Special Publication No. 25, 1959.

MIGRATION TRAILS

Lewis, Marcus W. *The Development of Early Emigrant Trails in the United States East of the Mississippi River.* 1933. Reprint. Washington, DC: National Genealogical Society Special Publication No. 3, 1962.

Wright, Norman E. "Settlement Patterns and Migration Routes." *Building an American Pedigree.* Provo, UT: Brigham Young University Press, 1969.

IMMIGRATIONS

Bristol and America. A Record of the First Settlers in the Colonies of North America, 1654–1685. Introduction by William Dodgson Bowman. Baltimore: Genealogical Publishing Co., 1970.

Cameron, Viola R. *Emigrants from Scotland to America, 1774–1775.* Baltimore: Genealogical Publishing Co., 1965.

Colket, Jr., Meredith B. *Founders of Early American Families: Emigrants from Europe 1607–1657.* Cleveland: Order of Founders and Patriots of America, 1975.

DeVille, Winston. *Gulf Coast Colonials: A Compendium of French Families in Early Eighteenth Century Louisiana.* Baltimore: Genealogical Publishing Co., 1968.

Faust, Albert B., and Gaius M. Brumbaugh. *Lists of Swiss Emigrants in the Eighteenth Century to the American Colonies.* Reprint (2 vols. in 1). Baltimore: Genealogical Publishing Co., 1968.

Geue, Chester W., and Ethel H. Geue. *A New Land Beckoned; German*

Immigration to Texas, 1844–1847. Fort Worth: Privately published, 1966.

Geue, Ethel H. *New Homes in a New Land; German Immigration to Texas, 1847–1861.* Waco: Privately published, 1970.

Giuseppi, M.S. *Naturalizations of Foreign Protestants in the American and West Indiana Colonies (Pursuant to Statute 13 George II, c. 7.)* Baltimore: Genealogical Publishing Co., 1964.

Hotten, John C. *The Original Lists of Persons of Quality, Emigrants, Religious Exiles, Political Rebels, Serving Men Sold for a Term of Years, Apprentices, Children Stolen, Maidens Pressed, and Others Who Went from Great Britain to the American Plantations, 1600–1700.* Baltimore: Genealogical Publishing Co., 1968.

Kaminkow, Jack, and Marion Kaminkow. *A List of Emigrants from England to America, 1718–1759.* Baltimore: Magna Charta Book Co., 1964.

Kaminkow, Marion J. *Original Lists of Emigrants in Bondage from London to the American Colonies, 1719–1744.* Baltimore: Magna Carta Book Co., 1967.

Knittle, Walter Allen. *Early Eighteenth Century Palatine Emigration.* Baltimore: Genealogical Publishing Co., 1965.

Lancour, Harold. *A Bibliography of Ship Passenger Lists, 1538–1825. Being a Guide to Published Lists of Early Immigrants to North America.* 3rd. rev. ed. by Richard J. Wolfe. New York: New York Public Library, 1966.

Munroe, J.B. *A List of Alien Passengers from January 1, 1847, to January 1, 1851, for the Use of the Overseers of the Poor.* [Boston]. 1851. Reprint. Baltimore: Genealogical Publishing Co., 1971.

Myers, Albert Cook. *Immigration of the Irish Quakers into Pennsylvania, 1682–1750.* Baltimore: Genealogical Publishing Co., 1969.

Olsson, Nils William. *Swedish Passenger Arrivals in New York, 1820–1850.* Chicago: Swedish Pioneer Historical Society, 1967.

Reaman, G. Elmore. *The Trail of the Huguenots in Europe, the United States, South Africa, and Canada.* Baltimore: Genealogical Publishing Co., 1972.

Rubincam, Milton. *Addenda et corrigenda to the Trail of the Huguenots in Europe, the United States, South Africa and Canada* by G. Elmore Reaman. Baltimore: Genealogical Publishing Co., 1972.

Rubincam, Milton. "Additional Corrections." *National Genealogical Society Quarterly* 53 (March 1965): 65–67.

Schelbert, Leo. "Notes on Swiss Emigrants." *National Geneological Society Quarterly* 60 (March 1972): 36–46. Corrections and additions to Faust and Brumbaugh.

Stephenson, Jean. *Scotch-Irish Migration to South Carolina, 1772: The Rev. William Martin and His Five Shiploads of Settlers.* Washington, DC: Privately published, 1972.

Strassburger, Ralph B. *Pennsylvania German Pioneers: A Publication of the Original Lists of Arrivals in the Port of Philadelphia from 1727 to 1808.* Edited by William J. Hinke. Reprint (omits Vol. 2). Baltimore: Genealogical Publishing Co., 1966.

Tepper, Michael, ed. *Emigrants to Pennsylvania, 1641–1819.* Baltimore: Genealogical Publishing Co., 1976.

Villeré, Sidney L.. *The Canary Islands Migration to Louisiana, 1778–1783. The History and Passenger Lists of the Isleños Volunteer Recruits and Their Families.* Baltimore: Genealogical Publishing Co., 1972.

Welcome Society of Pennsylvania. *Penn's Colony: Genealogical and Historical Materials Relating to the Settlement of Pennsylvania.* Vol. 1 edited by Walter Lee Sheppard, Jr. Vol. 2 edited by George E. McCracken. Baltimore: Genealogical Publishing Co., 1970.

COLLECTED PEDIGREES—SOUTH

Armstrong, Zella, comp. *Notable Southern Families.* Reprint (6 vols. in 3). Baltimore: Genealogical Publishing Co., 1947.

Boddie, John Bennett, comp. *Historical Southern Families.* vols. 1–19. Baltimore: Genealogical Publishing Co., 1967–.

Boddie, John Bennett, comp. *Southside Virginia Families.* 2 vols. Redwood City, CA: Pacific Coast Publishers, 1955–56.

Boddie, John Bennett, comp. *Virginia Historical Genealogies.* Redwood City, CA: Pacific Coast Publishers, 1954.

Crozier, William Armstrong. *A Key to Southern Pedigrees.* Baltimore: Southern Book Co., 1953.

Hardy, Stella P. *Colonial Families of the Southern States of America.* Baltimore: Genealogical Publishing Co., 1968.

INDIVIDUAL STATES

FLORIDA

Avant, David A., *Florida Pioneers and Their Alabama, Georgia, Carolina, Maryland and Virginia Ancestors.* Tallahassee, FL: Privately published, 1974.

VIRGINIA

Jester, Annie Lash, ed. *Adventurers of Purse and Person, Virginia, 1607–1625.* 2nd ed. Richmond: Privately published, 1964.

Stewart, Robert Armistead. *Index to Printed Virginia Genealogies.* Baltimore: Genealogical Publishing Co., 1965.

SURNAMES

American Council of Learned Societies. *Surnames in the United States Census of 1790; an Analysis of National Origins of the Population.* Baltimore: Genealogical Publishing Co., 1969.

Bailey, Rosalie Fellows. *Dutch Systems in Family Naming: New York, New Jersey.* Washington, DC: National Genealogical Society Special Publication No. 12, 1954.

Bardsley, C. W. *A Dictionary of English and Welsh Surnames, with Special American Instances.* Baltimore: Genealogical Publishing Co., 1967.

Black, George Fraser. *The Surnames of Scotland.* New York: New York Public Library, 1974.

Dolan, J. R. *English Ancestral Names: The Evolution of the Surname from Medieval Occupations.* New York: Clarkson N. Potter, 1972.

Ewen, C. L'Estrange. *A History of Surnames of the British Isles; A Concise Account of their Origin, Evolution, Etymology, and Legal Status.* Baltimore: Genealogical Publishing Co., 1968.

Fucilla, Joseph G. *Our Italian Surnames.* Evanston, IL: Chandler's, Inc., 1949.

MacLysaght, Edward. *The Surnames of Ireland.* New York: Barnes & Noble, 1970.

Maduell, Charles R. *The Romance of Spanish Surnames.* New Orleans: Privately published, 1967.

Reaney, P. H. *A Dictionary of British Surnames.* London: Routledge and Kegan Paul, 1970.

Reaney, P. H. *The Origin of English Surnames.* New York: Barnes and Noble, 1967.

Smith, Elsdon C. *Dictionary of American Family Names.* New York: Harper, 1975.

OTHER SOURCES CITED IN THE TEXT

Black, Henry Campbell. *Black's Law Dictionary.* 4th rev. ed. St. Paul, MN: West Publishing Co., 1968.

Brigham, Clarence S. *History and Bibliography of American Newspapers, 1690–1820.* 2 vols. Worcester, MA: American Antiquarian Society, 1947.

Brigham, Clarence S. *Additions and Corrections.* Worcester, MA: American Antiquarian Society, 1961.

Dictionary of American Biography. Under the auspices of the American Council of Learned Societies. New York: Charles Scribner's Sons, 1928–.

Directory: Historical Societies and Agencies in the United States and

Canada. 10th ed. Nashville: American Association for State and Local History, 1975.

Dubester, Henry J. *State Censuses: An Annotated Bibliography.* New York: B. Franklin, 1969.

Encyclopedia of American Biography. New York: American Historical Co., 1934–.

Franklin, W. Neil. *Federal Population and Mortality Schedules, 1790– 1890, in the National Archives and the States.* Washington, DC: National Archives, 1971.

Fries, Adelaide L., ed. and tr. *Records of the Moravians in North Carolina.* 9 vols. Publications of the North Carolina Historical Commission. Raleigh: Edwards & Broughton Printing Co., 1922–1954.

Gregory, Winifred, ed. *American Newspapers 1821–1936: A Union List of Files Available in the United States and Canada.* New York: H.W. Wilson Co., 1937.

The Hereditary Register of the United States of America. Washington, DC: United States Hereditary Register, Inc., 1972.

Jackson, Ronald V., and G. R. Teeples. (Computerized Indexes of U.S. Decennial Census Population Schedules). Provo, UT: Accelerated Indexing Systems, 1972–.

Meyer, Mary K. *Directory of Genealogical Societies and Periodicals.* Baltimore: Privately published, 1976.

National Cyclopedia of American Biography. Clifton, NJ: James T. White & Co., 1893–.

U.S. Bureau of the Census. *A Century of Population Growth from the First Census of the United States to the Twelfth, 1790–1900.* Washington, DC: Government Printing Office, 1909.

U.S. Library of Congress. *National Union Catalog of Manuscript Collections.* Washington, DC: Library of Congress, 1962–.

U.S. Library of Congress. *Newspapers in Microform, United States, 1948–1972* (formerly *Newspapers on Microfilm*). Washington, DC: Library of Congress, 1973.

Who Was Who in America, with World Notables (1942–1973). 5 vols. Chicago: A.N. Marquis Co.

Who's Who in America (1900–1974). 38 vols. Chicago: A.N. Marquis Co.

RESEARCH AIDS FOR INDIVIDUAL REGIONS & STATES—REGIONAL

National Genealogical Society. *Special Aids to Genealogical Research in Northeastern and Central States.* Washington: National Genealogical Society Special Publication No. 16., 1962.

National Genealogical Society. *Special Aids to Genealogical Research on Southern Families.* Washington: National Genealogical Society Special Publication No. 15., 1962.

St. Louis Genealogical Society. *Tracing Family Trees in Eleven States.* St. Louis: St. Louis Genealogical Society, 1970.

Wright, Norman E. *North American Genealogical Sources.* Provo, UT: Brigham Young University Press, 1968.

ALABAMA

Stephenson, Jean. "Alabama." *Genealogical Research* 2. Edited by Kenn Stryker-Rodda. Washington, DC: Privately published, 1971.

Webb, Mary Frances. "Alabama—Its Development and Records." *National Genealogical Society Quarterly* 57 (March 1969): 3–12.

ALASKA

Lada-Mocarski, Valerian, ed. *Bibliography of Books on Alaska Published before 1868.* New Haven: Yale University Press, 1969.

ARIZONA

Pare, Madeline F. *Arizona: A Student's Guide to Localized History.* New York: Teachers College Press, 1969.

ARKANSAS

Consult *Arkansas Family Historian,* Box 1033, Conway, AR 72032, and *The Backtracker,* Northwest Arkansas Genealogical Society, P.O. Box 362, Rogers, AR 72756.

CALIFORNIA

Rocq, Margaret M., ed. *California Local History: Bibliography and Union List of Library Holdings.* 2nd ed. Stanford: Stanford University Press, 1970.

Rolle, Andrew. *California: A Student's Guide to Localized History.* New York: Teachers College Press, 1965.

Rolle, Andrew. *Los Angeles: A Student's Guide to Localized History.* New York: Teachers College Press, 1965.

COLORADO

Ubbelohde, Carl W. *Colorado: A Student's Guide to Localized History.* New York: Teachers College Press, 1965.

CONNECTICUT

Barlow, Claude W. *Sources for Genealogical Searching in Connecticut and Massachusetts.* Syracuse: Central New York Genealogical Society, 1973.

Jacobus, Donald L. "Connecticut." *Genealogical Research Methods and Sources.* Edited by Milton Rubincam. Washington, DC: Privately published, 1960.

DELAWARE

DeValinger, Leon Jr. "Delaware." *Genealogical Research Methods and Sources.* Edited by Milton Rubincam. Washington, DC: Privately published. 1960.

Munroe, John A. *Delaware: A Student's Guide to Localized History.* New York: Teachers College Press, 1965.

Rubincam, Milton. *Pennsylvania and Delaware.* Salt Lake City: Genealogical Society of the Church of Jesus Christ of the Latter Day Saints, 1969.

DISTRICT OF COLUMBIA

Babbel, June Andrew. *Lest We Forget: A Guide to Genealogical Research in the Nation's Capital.* 2nd ed. Arlington, VA: Potomac Stake of Latter Day Saints, 1965.

FLORIDA

Florida State Library. *Genealogy and Local History: a Bibliography.* 5th ed. Tallahassee: Florida State Library, 1975.

Harris, Michael F. *Florida History: A Bibliography.* Metuchen, NJ: Scarecrow Press, 1972.

GEORGIA

Bonner, James C. *Georgia: A Student's Guide to Localized History.* New York: Teachers College Press, 1965.

Bryan, Mary Givens. "Genealogical Research in Georgia." *National Genealogical Society Quarterly* 40 (June 1952): 37–49.

Rowland, Arthui Ray. *A Bibliography of the Writings on Georgia History.* Hamden, CT: Shoe String Press, 1966.

Warren, Mary B. *Georgia Genealogical Bibliography.* Danielsville, GA: Heritage Papers, 1969.

HAWAII

Judd, Gerrit P. *Hawaii: A Student's Guide to Local History.* New York: Teachers College Press, 1965.

IDAHO

Wells, Merle W. *Idaho: A Student's Guide to Localized History.* New York: Teachers College Press, 1965.

ILLINOIS

Foster, Olive S. *Illinois: A Student's Guide to Localized History.* New York: Teachers College Press, 1968.

Parker, Jimmy B. "Illinois." *Genealogical Research* 2. Edited by Kenn Stryker- Rodda. Washington, DC: Privately published, 1971.

Volkel, Lowell M. "Genealogy in Illinois." *National Genealogical Society Quarterly* 63 (September 1975): 163–171.

INDIANA

McCay, Betty L. *Sources for Genealogical Searching in Indiana.* 2nd rev. ed. Indianapolis: Privately published, 1973.

Miller, Carolynne Wendel. *Aids for Genealogical Researching in Indiana.* Rev. ed. Detroit: Detroit Society for Genealogical Research, 1970.

Miller, Carolynne Wendel. "Indiana." *Genealogical Research* 2. Edited by Kenn Stryker-Rodda. Washington, DC: Privately published, 1971.

IOWA

McCracken, George E. "Iowa." *Genealogical Research* 2. Edited by Kenn Stryker-Rodda. Washington, DC: Privately published, 1971.

KANSAS

Miller, Nyle H. *Kansas: A Student's Guide to Localized History.* New York: Teachers College Press, 1965.

KENTUCKY

Burns, Annie Walker. *Aids to Genealogical Research in Kentucky.* Washington: National Genealogical Society Special Publication No. 15, 1957.

Clark, Thomas D. *Kentucky: A Student's Guide to Localized History.* New York: Teachers College Press, 1965.

Dorman, John F. "Kentucky." *Genealogical Research* 2. Edited by Kenn Stryker-Rodda. Washington, DC: Privately published, 1971.

Dorman, John F. *Some Sources for Kentucky Genealogical Research.* Washington, DC: National Genealogical Society Special Publication No. 15, 1957.

Hardin, Bayless E. *Genealogical Research in Kentucky.* Washington, DC: National Genealogical Society Special Publication No. 15, 1957.

Hinds, Charles F. "Kentucky Records, How to Use Them and Where They Are Located." *National Genealogical Society Quarterly* 59 (March 1971): 3–7.

LOUISIANA

DeVille, Winston. "Louisiana." *Genealogical Research* 2. Edited by Kenn Stryker-Rodda. Washington, DC: Privately published, 1971.

Taylor, Joe Gray. *Louisiana: A Student's Guide to Localized History.* New York: Teachers College Press, 1966.

MAINE

Davis, Walter G. "Maine and New Hampshire." *Genealogical Research Methods and Sources.* Edited by Milton Rubincam. Washington, DC: Privately published, 1960.

Fisher, Carleton E. "Research in Maine." *National Genealogical Society Quarterly* 55 (March 1967): 83–88.

MARYLAND

Brown, Mary Ross. *An Illustrated Genealogy of the Counties of Maryland and the District of Columbia as a Guide to Locating Records.* Baltimore: Maryland Historical Society, 1967.

Manakee, Harold R. *Maryland: A Student's Guide to Localized History.* New York: Teachers College Press, 1968.

Meyer, Mary K. *Genealogical Research in Maryland: A Guide.* Baltimore: Maryland Historical Society, 1976.

MASSACHUSETTS

Barlow, Claude W. *Sources for Genealogical Searching in Connecticut and Massachusetts.* Syracuse, NY: Central New York Genealogical Society, 1973.

Bowen, Richard LeBaron. *Massachusetts Records: A Handbook for Genealogists, Historians, Lawyers, and Other Researchers.* Boston: Privately published, 1957.

Holman, Winifred L. "Massachusetts." *Genealogical Research Methods and Sources*. Edited by Milton Rubincam, Washington, DC: Privately published, 1960.

Reid, William J. *Massachusetts: A Student's Guide to Localized History*. New York: Teachers College Press, 1965.

Michigan

Harmison, Eva M. "Michigan." *Genealogical Research* 2. Edited by Kenn Stryker-Rodda, Washington, DC: Privately published, 1971.

Michigan Historical Commission. *Michigan Bibliography*. Compiled by Floyd B. Streeter. 2 vols. Lansing: Michigan Historical Commission, 1921.

Minnesota

Brook, Michael. *Reference Guide to Minnesota History: A Subject Bibliography of Books, Pamphlets, and Articles in English*. St. Paul: Minnesota Historical Society, 1974.

Fridley, Russell W. *Minnesota: A Student's Guide to Localized History*. New York: Teachers College Press, 1966.

Mississippi

Lackey, Richard S. "Mississippi." *Genealogical Research* 2. Edited by Kenn Stryker-Rodda, Washington, DC: Privately published, 1971.

Mississippi Genealogical Society. *Survey of Records in Mississippi Court Houses*. Jackson, MS: Mississippi Genealogical Society, 1957.

Moore, John H., and Margaret D. Moore. *Mississippi: A Student's Guide to Localized History*. New York: Teachers College Press, 1970.

Missouri

Williams, Betty H., and Jacqueline H. Williams. *Resources for Genealogical Research in Missouri*. Warrensburg, MO: Privately published, 1969.

Montana

Brown, Margery H., and Virginia G. Griffing. *Montana: A Student's Guide to Localized History*. New York: Teachers College Press, 1971.

Nebraska

North Platte Genealogical Society Newsletter. 820 W. 4th Street, North Platte, NE 79101.

NEVADA

Elliott Russell R., and Helen J. Poulton. *Writings on Nevada: A Selected Bibliography*. Reno: University of Nevada Press, 1963.

NEW HAMPSHIRE

Davis, Walter G. "Maine and New Hampshire." *Genealogical Research Methods and Sources*. Edited by Milton Rubincam, Washington, DC: Privately published, 1960.

Squires, James D. *New Hampshire: A Student's Guide to Localized History*. New York: Teachers College Press, 1966.

Towle, Laird. *New Hampshire Genealogical Research Guide*. Bowie, MD: Privately published, 1973.

NEW JERSEY

Genealogical Society of New Jersey. *Genealogical Research: A Guide to Source Material in the Archives and History Bureau of the New Jersey State Library*. Trenton, NJ: Archives and History Bureau, 1971.

Rubincam, Milton. "New Jersey." *Genealogical Research Methods and Sources*. Edited by Milton Rubincam, Washington, DC: Privately published, 1960.

Stryker-Rodda, Kenn. *New Jersey: Digging for Ancestors in the Garden State*. Detroit: Detroit Society for Genealogical Research, 1970.

Williams, Ethel W. "Research in New Jersey." *Know Your Ancestors*. Rutland, VT: Charles E. Tuttle Co., 1960.

NEW MEXICO

Forrest, James Taylor. *New Mexico: A Student's Guide to Localized History*. New York: Teachers College Press, 1971.

Consult also *New Mexico Genealogist*, P.O. Box 8734, Albuquerque, NM 87108.

NEW YORK

Bailey, Rosalie Fellows. *Guide to Genealogical and Biographical Sources for New York City (Manhattan), 1783–1898*. New York: Privately published, 1954.

Nestler, Harold. *A Bibliography of New York State Communities, Counties, Towns, Villages*. Port Washington, NY: I. J. Friedman, 1968.

Rubincam, Milton. "New York City." *Genealogical Research Methods and Sources*. Edited by Milton Rubincam, Washington, DC: Privately published, 1960.

Seversmith, Herbert F. "Long Island." *Genealogical Research Methods and Sources*. Edited by Milton Rubincam, Washington, DC: Privately published, 1960.

Seversmith, Herbert F., and Kenn Stryker-Rodda. *Long Island Genealogical Source Material: A Bibliography*. Washington, DC: National Genealogical Society Special Publication No. 24, 1962.

Sibley, Mary J. "Upstate New York." *Genealogical Research Methods and Sources*. Edited by Milton Rubincam, Washington, DC: Privately published, 1960.

Still, Bayard. *New York City: A Student's Guide to Localized History*. New York: Teachers College Press, 1965.

Williams, Ethel W. "Trailing Ancestors Through New York State." *Know Your Ancestors*. Rutland, VT: Charles E. Tuttle Co., 1960.

North Carolina

Draughon, Wallace R., and William P. Johnson. *North Carolina Genealogical Reference: A Research Guide*. 2nd ed. Durham, NC: Privately published, 1966.

McCay, Betty L. *Sources for Genealogical Searching in North Carolina*. Indianapolis: Privately published, 1969.

Powell, William S. *North Carolina: A Student's Guide to Localized History*. New York: Teachers College Press, 1965.

Powell, William S. *North Carolina County Histories: A Bibliography*. Chapel Hill: University of North Carolina Press, 1958.

Powell, William S. *Raleigh-Durham-Chapel Hill: A Student's Guide to Localized History*. New York: Teachers College Press, 1968.

Stephenson, Jean. "North Carolina." *Genealogical Research Methods and Sources*. Edited by Milton Rubincam, Washington, DC: Privately published, 1960.

North Dakota

Consult *Black Hills Nuggets*, P.O. Box 1495, Rapid City, SD 57701.

Ohio

Douthit, Ruth L. "Ohio." *Genealogical Research 2*. Edited by Kenn Stryker-Rodda. Washington, DC: Privately published, 1971.

Douthit, Ruth L. *Ohio Resources for Genealogists*. Rev. ed. Detroit: Detroit Society for Genealogical Research, 1971.

Tucker, Louis L. *Cincinnati: A Student's Guide to Localized History*. New York: Teachers College Press, 1969.

Weisenburger, Francis P. *Ohio: A Student's Guide to Localized History*. New York: Teachers College Press, 1965.

Williams, Ethel W. "Ansearchin' Through Ohio." *Know Your Ancestors*. Rutland, VT: Charles E. Tuttle Co., 1960.

OKLAHOMA

Gibson, Arrell M. *Oklahoma: A Student's Guide to Localized History*. New York: Teachers College Press, 1965.
Also consult *Oklahoma Genealogical Society Quarterly*, P.O. Box 314, Oklahoma City, OK 73101.

OREGON

Duniway, David C. *Have You an Oregon Ancestor*. Salem, OR: Oregon State Archives, 1962.
"Genealogical Research in Oregon." *National Genealogical Society Quarterly* 47 (September 1959): 115-128.
Oregon Historical Society. *Microfilm Guide* (to genealogical and historical records and materials). Portland, OR: Privately published, 1973.
Also consult *Oregon Genealogical Society Bulletin*, P.O. Box 1214, Eugene, OR 97401, and *Genealogical Forum of Portland Monthly Bulletin*, 1410 SW Morrison, Room 812, Portland, OR 97204.

PENNSYLVANIA

Hoenstine, Floyd G. *Guide to Genealogical and Historical Research in Pennsylvania*. 2nd rev. ed. Hollidaysburg, PA: Privately published, 1966.
McCay, Betty L. *Sources for Genealogical Searching in Pennsylvania*. 3rd rev. ed. Indianapolis: Privately published, 1973.
Pennsylvania Historical and Museum Commission. *Preliminary Guide to the Research Materials of the Pennsylvania Historical and Museum Commission*. Harrisburg, PA: Pennsylvania Historical and Museum Commission, 1959.
Rubincam, Milton. "Pennsylvania." *Genealogical Research Methods and Sources*. Edited by Milton Rubincam. Washington, DC: Privately published, 1960.
Rubincam, Milton. *Pennsylvania and Delaware*. Salt Lake City: Genealogical Society of the Church of Jesus Christ of Latter Day Saints, 1969.
Stevens, Sylvester K. *Pennsylvania: A Student's Guide to Localized History*. New York: Teachers College Press, 1965.
Stevens, Sylvester K., and Donald H. Kent. *County Government and Archives in Pennsylvania*. Harrisburg, PA: Pennsylvania Historical and Museum Commission, 1947.

Williams, Ethel W. "Keys to the Keystone State." *Know Your Ancestors*. Rutland, VT: Charles E. Tuttle Co., 1975.

RHODE ISLAND

Farnham, Charles W. *Rhode Island Colonial Records*. Salt Lake City: Genealogical Society of the Church of Jesus Christ of the Latter Day Saints, 1969.

Monahon, Clifford P. *Rhode Island: A Student's Guide to Localized History*. New York: Teachers College Press, 1965.

West, Edward H. "Rhode Island." *Genealogical Research Methods and Sources*. Edited by Milton Rubincam. Washington, DC: Privately published, 1960.

SOUTH CAROLINA

Moore, John Hammond. *Research Materials in South Carolina*. Columbia, SC: University of South Carolina Press, 1967.

Stephenson, Jean. "South Carolina." *Genealogical Research Methods and Sources*. Edited by Milton Rubincam, Washington, DC: Privately published, 1960.

Wakefield, Roberta P. "Genealogical Source Materials in South Carolina." Washington, DC: National Genealogical Society Special Publication No. 15, 1957.

SOUTH DAKOTA

Schell, Herbert. *South Dakota: A Student's Guide to Localized History*. New York: Teachers College Press, 1971.

Consult also *Black Hills Nuggets*, P.O. Box 1495, Rapid City, SD 57701.

TENNESSEE

Alderson, William T. *Tennessee: A Student's Guide to Localized History*. New York: Teachers College Press, 1965.

Cram, Kendall J. *Guide to the Use of Genealogical Material in the Tennessee State Library and Archives*. Rev. ed. Nashville: Tennessee State Library and Archives, 1966.

McBride, Robert M. "Tennessee." *Genealogical Research 2*. Edited by Kenn Stryker-Rodda, Washington, DC: Privately published, 1971.

McCay, Betty L. *Sources for Genealogical Searching in Tennessee*. Indianapolis: Privately published, 1970.

TEXAS

Frantz, Joe B. *Houston: A Student's Guide to Localized History.* New York: Teachers College Press, 1971.

Osburn, Mary. "Outline of Sources for Genealogical Research in the Texas State Archives." *Local History and Genealogical Society* 15 (1969): 2ff.

Winfrey, Gorman. "'Gone to Texas': Sources for Genealogical Research in the Lone Star State." *Stirpes* 9 (1969): 87–95.

UTAH

Cooley, Everett L. *Utah: A Student's Guide to Localized History.* New York: Teachers College Press, 1968.

Jaussi, Laureen D., and Gloria D. Chaston. *Genealogical Records of Utah.* Provo, UT: Privately published, 1974.

Wright, Norman E. "Using Selected LDS and Early Utah Sources." *Building an American Pedigree.* Provo, UT: Brigham Young University Press, 1974.

VERMONT

Stephenson, Jean. "Vermont." *Genealogical Research Methods and Sources.* Edited by Milton Rubincam, Washington, DC: Privately published, 1960.

Stillwell, Lewis D. *Migration from Vermont.* Montpelier, VT: Vermont Historical Society, 1948.

VIRGINIA

Hiden, Martha W. "Virginia." *Genealogical Research Methods and Sources.* Edited by Milton Rubincam. Washington, DC: Privately published, 1960.

Livingston, Virginia P. *Some Peculiarities of Genealogical Research in Virginia.* Salt Lake City: Genealogical Society of the Church of Jesus Christ of the Latter Day Saints, 1969.

McCay, Betty L. *Sources for Genealogical Searching in Virginia and West Virginia.* Indianapolis: Privately published, 1971.

Stewart, Robert A. *Index to Printed Virginia Genealogies: Including Key and Bibliography.* Reprint. Baltimore: Genealogical Publishing Co., 1965.

Swem, Earl G. *Virginia Historical Index.* Reprint (2 vols. in 4). Gloucester, MA: Peter Smith, 1965.

WASHINGTON

Consult *Seattle Genealogical Society Bulletin*, P.O. Box 549, Seattle, WA 98111.

WEST VIRGINIA

McCay, Betty L. *Sources for Genealogical Searching in Virginia and West Virginia*. Indianapolis: Privately published, 1971.

Munn, Robert F. *Index to West Virginiana*. Charleston, WV: Education Foundation, 1960.

WISCONSIN

Doane, Gilbert H. "Wisconsin." *Genealogical Research 2*. Edited by Kenn Stryker-Rodda, Washington, DC: Privately published, 1971.

Gleason, Margaret. *Printed Resources for Genealogical Searching in Wisconsin: A Selective Bibliography*. Detroit: Detroit Society for Genealogical Research, 1964.

Platt, Doris H. *Wisconsin: A Student's Guide to Localized History*. New York: Teachers College Press, 1965.

WYOMING

Homsher, Lola M. *Wyoming: A Student's Guide to Localized History*. New York: Teachers College Press, 1966.

PERIODICALS—GENERAL LIST

Daughters of the American Revolution Magazine (Genealogical Department). 1776 D Street, NW, Washington, DC 20006.

Genealogical Helper. P.O. Box 368, Logan, UT 84321.

Genealogical Periodical Annual Index (GPAI). Laird C. Towle, ed., 3602 Maureen Lane, Bowie, MD 20715.

Mayflower Quarterly. 128 Massasoit Dr., Warwick, RI 02888.

National Genealogical Society Quarterly (NGSQ). 1921 Sunderland Place, N.W., Washington, DC 20036.

New England Historical and Genealogical Register (Register). 101 Newbury St., Boston, MA 02116.

Prologue, The Journal of the National Archives. National Archives, Washington, DC 20408.

Southern Genealogist's Exchange Quarterly (SGEQ). 4305 Coquina Dr., Jacksonville, FL 32250.

The American Genealogist (TAG). George E. McCracken, ed., 1232 39th St., Des Moines, IA 50311.

ALABAMA

Alabama Genealogical Society, Inc., Magazine. 2 Brantwood Drive, Montgomery, AL 36109.

Deep South Genealogical Quarterly. Mobile Genealogical Society, Inc., P.O. Box 6224, Mobile, AL 36606.

Northeast Alabama Settlers. Northeast Alabama Genealogical Society, Inc., P.O. Box 674, Gadsden, AL 35902.

Pioneer Trails. Birmingham Genealogical Society, Inc., 1028 Montclair Rd., Birmingham, AL 35213.

Tap Roots. Genealogical Society of East Alabama, Inc., Box 45, Hurtsboro, AL 36860.

Valley Leaves. Tennessee Valley Genealogical Society, P.O. Box 1512, Huntsville, AL 35807.

ARIZONA

Copper State Bulletin. Arizona State Genealogical Society, P.O. Box 6027, Tucson, AZ 85733.

ARKANSAS

Arkansas Family Historian. Box 1033, Conway, AR 72032.

The Backtracker. Northwest Arkansas Genealogical Society, P.O. Box 362, Rogers, AR 72756.

CALIFORNIA

Genealogical Goldmine. Paradise Genealogical Society, P.O. Box 335, Paradise, CA 95969.

Lifeliner. Genealogical Society of Riverside, P.O. Box 2664, Riverside, CA 92506.

Orange County Genealogical Society Quarterly. P.O. Box 1587, Orange, CA 92668.

Searcher. Southern California Genealogical Society, P.O. Box 7665, Bixby Knolls Station, Long Beach, CA 90807.

COLORADO

Colorado Genealogist. Colorado Genealogical Society, P.O. Box 9654, Denver, CO 80209.

CONNECTICUT

Nutmegger. Connecticut Society of Genealogists, 16 Royal Oak Drive, West Hartford, CT 06107.

Stamford Genealogical Society Bulletin. P.O. Box 249, Stamford, CT 06904.

DELAWARE

Maryland and Delaware Genealogist. Box 352, St. Michaels, MD 21663.

FLORIDA

Ancestry. Palm Beach County Genealogical Society, P.O. Box 1746, West Palm Beach, FL 33402.

Florida Genealogical Journal. Florida Genealogical Society, Inc., P.O. Box 18624, Tampa, FL 33609.

GEORGIA

Georgia Genealogical Magazine. Rev. Silas E. Lucas, ed. P.O. Box 229, Easley, SC 29640.

Georgia Genealogical Society Quarterly. P.O. Box 4761, Atlanta, GA 30302.

Georgia Genealogist. Mary B. Warren, ed., Heritage Papers, Danielsville, GA 30633.

Georgia Pioneers Genealogical Magazine. P.O. Box 1028, Albany, GA 31702.

IDAHO

Idaho Genealogical Society Quarterly. 610 N. Julia Davis Dr., Boise, ID 83706.

ILLINOIS

Central Illinois Genealogical Quarterly. Box 2068, Decatur, IL 62526.

Chicago Genealogist. Chicago Genealogical Society, P.O. Box 1160, Chicago, IL 60690.

Gleanings. Bloomington-Normal Genealogical Society, P.O. Box 432, Normal, IL 61761.

Illiana Genealogist. Illiana Genealogical and Historical Society, Box 207, Danville, IL 61832.

Illinois State Genealogical Society Quarterly. P.O. Box 2225, Springfield, IL 62705.

INDIANA

Genealogy. Indiana Historical Society, 140 N. Senate Ave., Indianapolis, IN 46204.

Hoosier Genealogist. Indiana Historical Society, 140 N. Senate Ave., Indianapolis, IN 46204.

Illiana Genealogist. Illiana Genealogical and Historical Society, Box 207, Danville, IL 61832.

Michiana Searcher. Elkhart County Genealogical Society, 1812 Jean-wood Ave., Elkhart, IN 46514.
Tri-State Trader (Genealogical Department). P.O. Box 90, Knightstown, IN 46148.

IOWA

Hawkeye Heritage. P.O. Box 4084, Highland Park Station, Des Moines, IA 50333.

KANSAS

Kansas City Genealogist. 110 W. 36th St., Kansas City, KS 66106.
Kansas Kin. Riley County Genealogical Society, 909 Kearney St., Manhattan, KS 66502.
Midwest Genealogical Register. 2911 Rivera, Wichita, KS 67211.
Topeka Genealogical Society Quarterly. P.O. Box 4048, Topeka, KS 66604.
Treesearcher. Kansas Genealogical Society, Box 103, Dodge City, KS 67801.

KENTUCKY

East Kentuckian. Box 107, Stanville, KY 41659.
Kentucky Ancestors. Kentucky Historical Society, P.O. Box H, Frankfort, KY 40601.
Kentucky Family Records. P.O. Box 1465, Owensboro, KY 42301.
Kentucky Genealogist. Box 4894, Washington, DC 20008.

LOUISIANA

Ark-La-Tex Newsletter. P.O. Box 71, Shreveport, LA 71161.
Genealogical Register. Louisiana Genealogical and Historical Society, P.O. Box 3454, Baton Rouge, LA 70821.
New Orleans Genesis. P.O. Box 51791, New Orleans, LA 70151.

MAINE

Maine Genealogical Inquirer. Box 253, Oakland, ME 04963.

MARYLAND

Maryland and Delaware Genealogist. Box 352, St. Michaels, MD 21663.
Maryland Genealogical Society Bulletin. 201 W. Monument St., Baltimore, MD 21201.

MICHIGAN

Detroit Society for Genealogical Research Magazine. c/o Burton Histori-
cal Collection, Detroit Public Library, 5201 Woodward Ave. at
Kirby, Detroit, MI 48202.
Family Trails. Michigan Department of Education, Bureau of Li-
brary Services, 735 E. Michigan Ave., Lansing, MI 48913.
Flint Genealogical Quarterly. c/o Mrs. Maryann Homer, 1020 Perry,
Flint, MI 48504.
Michiana Searcher. Elkhart County Genealogical Society, 1812 Jean-
wood Ave., Elkhart, IN 46514.
Michigana. Western Michigan Genealogical Society, Library Plaza
NE, Grand Rapids, MI 49506.

MISSISSIPPI

Journal of Mississippi History, P.O. Box 571, Jackson, MS 39205.
Mississippi Coast Historical and Genealogical Society (Proceedings and
Journal). P.O. Box 513, Biloxi, MS 39530.
Mississippi Genealogical Exchange. P.O. Box 434, Forest, MS 39074.
Mississippi Genealogy and Local History. P.O. Box 9114, Shreveport, LA
71109.

MISSOURI

Kansas City Genealogist. 5645 Osage, Kansas City, KS 66106.
St. Louis Genealogical Society Quarterly. Suite 268, 1617 S. Brentwood
Blvd., St. Louis, MO 63144.

NEBRASKA

North Platte Genealogical Society Newsletter. 820 West 4th St., North
Platte, NE 69101.

NEW JERSEY

Genealogical Magazine of New Jersey. Box 1291, New Brunswick, NJ
08903.
New York Genealogical and Biographical Record. 122 E. 58th St., New
York, NY 10022.

NEW MEXICO

New Mexico Genealogist. Box 8734, Albuquerque, NM 87108.

NEW YORK

Mid-Hudson Genealogical Journal. 20 Styvestandt Drive, Poughkeep-
sie, NY 12601.

New York Genealogical and Biographical Record. 122 E. 58th St., New York, NY 10022.

Tree Talks. Central New York Genealogical Society, Box 104, Colvin Station, Syracuse, NY 13205.

Western New York Genealogical Society Journal. c/o Mrs. Harold J. Miller, 209 Nassau Ave., Kenmore, NY 14217.

NORTH CAROLINA

Carolina Genealogist. Mary B. Warren, ed., Heritage Papers, Danielsville, GA 30633.

North Carolina Genealogical Society Journal. P.O. Box 1492, Raleigh, NC 27602.

North Carolina Genealogy (formerly *The North Carolinian*). P.O. Box 1770, Raleigh, NC 27602.

OHIO

Gateway to the West. c/o Anita Short, Rt. 1, Arcanum, OH 45304.

Ohio Records and Pioneer Families. Ohio Genealogical Society, P.O. Box 2625, Mansfield, OH 44906.

OKLAHOMA

Oklahoma Genealogical Society Quarterly. P.O. Box 314, Oklahoma City, OK 73101.

Tulsa Annals. Tulsa Genealogical Society, P.O. Box 385, Tulsa, OK 74101.

OREGON

Genealogical Forum of Portland Bulletin. 1410 SW Morrison, Room 812, Portland, OR 97204.

Oregon Genealogical Society Bulletin. P.O. Box 1214, Eugene, OR 97401.

PENNSYLVANIA

Pennsylvania Genealogical Magazine. Pennsylvania Genealogical Society, 1300 Locust St., Philadelphia, PA 19107.

Pennsylvania Traveler. Box 307, Danboro, PA 18916.

SOUTH CAROLINA

Carolina Genealogist. Mary B. Warren, ed., Heritage Papers, Danielsville, GA 30633.

South Carolina Magazine of Ancestral Research. Laurence K. Wells, ed., Box 694, Kingstree, SC 29556.

SOUTH DAKOTA

Black Hills Nuggets. P.O. Box 1495, Rapid City, SD 57701.

TENNESSEE

Ansearchin' News. Tennessee Genealogical Society, P.O. Box 12124, Memphis, TN 38112.

Echoes from the East Tennessee Historical Society, Lawson McGhee Library, Knoxville, TN 37901.

Tennessee Historical Quarterly. 403 7th Ave. N., Nashville, TN 37219.

West Tennessee Historical Society Papers. P.O. Box 82260, Memphis State University, Memphis, TN 38152.

TEXAS

Austin Genealogical Society Quarterly. P.O. Box 774, Austin, TX 78767.

Central Texas Genealogical Society Quarterly. 1717 Austin Ave., Waco, TX 76701.

Foot Prints. Fort Worth Genealogical Society, P.O. Box 864, Fort Worth, TX 76101.

Genealogical Record. Houston Genealogical Forum, 7130 Evans, Houston, TX 77017.

Local History and Genealogical Society Quarterly. 8446 Santa Clara Drive, Dallas, TX 75218.

Mesquite Historical and Genealogical Society Quarterly. P.O. Box 165, Mesquite, TX 75149.

Our Heritage. San Antonio Genealogical and Historical Society, Box 6383, San Antonio, TX 78209.

South Texas Genealogical and Historical Society Quarterly. P.O. Box 40, Gonzales, TX 78629.

Stirpes. Texas State Genealogical Society, 2515 Sweetbrier Drive, Dallas, TX 75228.

Texas Heritage. Texas Family Heritage, Inc., c/o Patricia Chadwell, ed., P.O. Box 17007, Fort Worth, TX 76102.

Yellowed Pages. Southeast Texas Historical and Genealogical Society, 2870 Driftwood Lane, Beaumont, TX 77703.

VIRGINIA

Virginia Genealogical Society Quarterly. c/o Jefferson Hotel, Box 1397, Richmond, VA 23211.

The Virginia Genealogist. John F. Dorman, ed. Box 4883, Washington, DC 20008.

WASHINGTON

Eastern Washington Genealogical Society Bulletin. P.O. Box 1826, Spokane, WA 99210.

Seattle Genealogical Society Bulletin. Box 549, Seattle, WA 98111.

WEST VIRGINIA

West Virginia Echoer. 398 National Road, Wheeling, WV 26003.

WISCONSIN

M.C.G.W. Reporter. Milwaukee County Genealogical Society, Inc., 916 East Lyon Street, Milwaukee, WI 53202.

Wisconsin Helper. 2941 South 56th St., Milwaukee, WI 53219.

Wisconsin State Genealogical Society Newsletter. P.O. Box 90068, Milwaukee, WI 53202.

BOOK DEALERS

Banner Press, Inc., P.O. Box 20180, Birmingham, AL 35216.

Deseret Book Co., P.O. Box 659, Salt Lake City, UT 84110.

Genealogical Book Co., 521–523 St. Paul Place, Baltimore, MD 21202.

Goodspeed's Book Shop, 18 Beacon St., Boston, MA 02108.

Mrs. Donna Hotaling, Agent, 2255 Cedar Lane, Vienna, VA 22180. (Agent for American Society of Genealogists' publications.)

Charles E. Tuttle Co., Inc., Rutland, VT 05701.

Superintendent of Documents, Government Printing Office, Washington, DC 20402. (A few selected publications are available from local government bookstores.)

Index